GW01087160

MINI
The Book.

Contents

	7-24	**The New Millennium.**	What defines the spirit of an era? Which products will be tomorrow's classics? What kind of world did the MINI grow up in? A look back at the turn of the millennium.
	25-50	**Around the World.**	Ten photographers, creative designers and artists showcase the MINI as part of their world, their city, their style and their art.
	51-72	**Paul Smith, Mary Quant, MINI and the Swinging Sixties.**	The MINI was the icon of an era: London designers Paul Smith and Mary Quant on the wild side of the sixties and the MINI past and present.
	73-86	**The Legends.**	The history of the MINI is closely bound up with three men who turned a car into an enduring legend: a tale of three heroes.
	87-100	**The Oxbridge Race.**	When a moving story became an action thriller: the removals men had just 129 days to set up a new home for the MINI.
	101-130	**From the Original to the Original.**	The MINI design is unique – and has been since 1959. The much-loved original from the sixties was remoulded into a 21st-century original. And now it's time to welcome the new MINI.
	131-148	**Inspired by MINI.**	More than just a car, the MINI inspires artists, advertisers and fans in their constant quest for novel ideas. You name it, the MINI has probably done it.
	149-158	**MINI Community.**	Fans of the MINI have gelled into a genuine community. The MINI CHALLENGE sees professionals and MINI fans revving up on the race track, while gatherings such as MINI United pull in thousands of MINI enthusiasts.
	159-168	**Facts & Figures.**	A wealth of stories and anecdotes have grown up around the MINI. Here we offer a selection of the most dramatic and bizarre snippets from its history.
	169-187	**Technical Features. Timeline.**	There's more to MINI than meets the eye. From DSC to CBC, EBD to ASC+T, this glossary reveals the hidden secrets inside the MINI. And read on for a chronology of key events in the history of MINI … and the world.

1st edition 2006
Copyright © 2006 by BMW AG, Munich

Published by:
Bayerische Motoren Werke AG, Munich,
MINI Brand Management

Concept: Anne Urbauer
Editor-in-chief: Peter Würth
Art direction: Stefan Pietsch & Georgina Lim
Design assistant: Constanze Klingler
Final artwork: Kurt Wilhelm
Editorial staff: Christina Reiffert (managing director), Katja Gross (assistant)
Contributors: Joachim Bessing, Christian Geib, Peter Glaser, Cornelia Haff,
Sebastian Hammelehle, Marc van Huisseling, Jürgen Lewandowski,
Jürgen Pander, Christina Reiffert, Kristin Rübesamen, Alistair Weaver,
Peter Würth
Translators: Dr Sonia Brough, Philip Radcliffe, David Reinhart, Alan Seaton
Art Buying: Alexandra Dimitrijevic, Tamara Hansinger
Photographers and sources: see p. 190
Project managers: Ulrike Häubl, Alexander Lohmann, Dr Jessica Renndorfer
Production: Alfred Fürholzer (manager), Michael Robertson
Printing and binding: Kastner & Callwey Druck GmbH

Printed in Germany

International distribution:
Die Gestalten Verlag GmbH & Co. KG
www.die-gestalten.de

Produced by:
HOFFMANN UND CAMPE VERLAG GmbH, Hamburg
A company of GANSKE VERLAGSGRUPPE
Harvestehuder Weg 42
20149 Hamburg
www.hoffmann-und-campe.de

Distribution Germany, Austria, Switzerland:
HOFFMANN UND CAMPE VERLAG GmbH

ISBN 978-3-89955-180-8

HOFFMANN
UND CAMPE

A company of
GANSKE VERLAGSGRUPPE

The New Millennium.

2000-2010, the first decade of the new millennium. What defines the spirit and aesthetic sensibilities of this era? Which products are destined to become future classics? Despite widely differing design vocabularies and forms of expression, a clutch of recognisably global phenomena stand out. Digital information is sent around the world at the click of a mouse button, logistics and transport are one of the key priorities of our time. By teaming up with artists and designers, traditional businesses are turning into new "it" labels. Multifunctional gadgets and gizmos are responding to accelerating change while geographically rooted social communities are splintering into global subcultures with their own individual language of communication. Design is breaking the bounds of plain functionality in order to remain competitive in a saturated market, limited editions and countertrends are lending objects cult status. Disciplines are intersecting and merging into cross-genre artworks that fuse fashion and music, art and design, architecture and narrative. Here is a portfolio from the time of birth of the new MINI.

Getting personal

Z.Island
Zaha Hadid with Ernestomeda
Italy, 2006

The Z.Island prototype by DuPont
Corian offers a wealth of choices

Adicolor
Adidas
Germany, 2006

The Adicolor shoe concept from the
Adidas Originals collection panders
to the irrepressible urge to express
one's personality and individual identity. Using different styling tools, from
felt tip to spray can, everyone can
create their very own personalised
shoe.

Aibo
Sony
Japan, 2005

Staying mobile

Frog Line
Mandarina Duck
Italy, 2000

Frog Line by Mandarina Duck is tailored to the requirements of modern nomads who are not rooted to any particular spot in the big wide world. Aluminium elements make them extremely light, while the polypropylene cover is both durable and expandable.

PAL
Henry Kloss and Tom de Vesto
for Tivoli Audio
USA, 2001

It's the antithesis of complex electronic products. With the outdoor radio PAL, hi-fi pioneer Henry Kloss has combined high-performance technology with user-friendly simplicity. The weatherproof, fifties-style plastic casing features a stereo-aux plug which can be connected to CD as well as MP3 players.

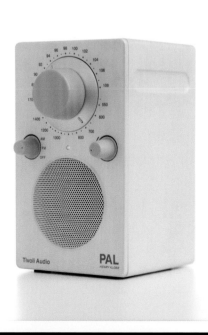

The 36-square-metre cube made
utopian living a reality in 2006. The
Loftcube generates much-needed
space in increasingly crowded urban
areas. Placed in position by crane or
helicopter on the flat roof of a building and connected to its energy sup-
ply, this mobile home bids farewell to
packing boxes.

U2 iPod
Jonathan Ive for Apple
USA, 2004

The icon of the digital music era was
first introduced in 2001. Since then
the iPod family has been joined by
the Mini, Shuffle and Nano, as well as
special editions such as the U2 iPod
featuring the band members' signa-
tures. An easy-to-operate menu gives
access to a maximum 80 GB of
songs, photos, podcasts and videos.

Digilux 2
Achim Heine for Leica

Englishman Nicholas Roope has revived a popular forties icon. Equipped with the latest technology and a Bluetooth option, the retro telephone receivers can be connected to a mobile phone as the headset or to a computer for VoIP calls. It reduces radiation by 90 percent.

Multipurposeful

Algues
Ronan & Erwan Bouroullec
for Vitra
Switzerland, 2005

The Algues (facing page) have been
conceived both as decorative elements and as basic building blocks of
interior design. Packed as a single 32
x 26 cm unit, the pieces of plastic
algae can be linked together to create a weblike structure – from a fili-
gree curtain to an opaque room
divider creating temporary spaces.

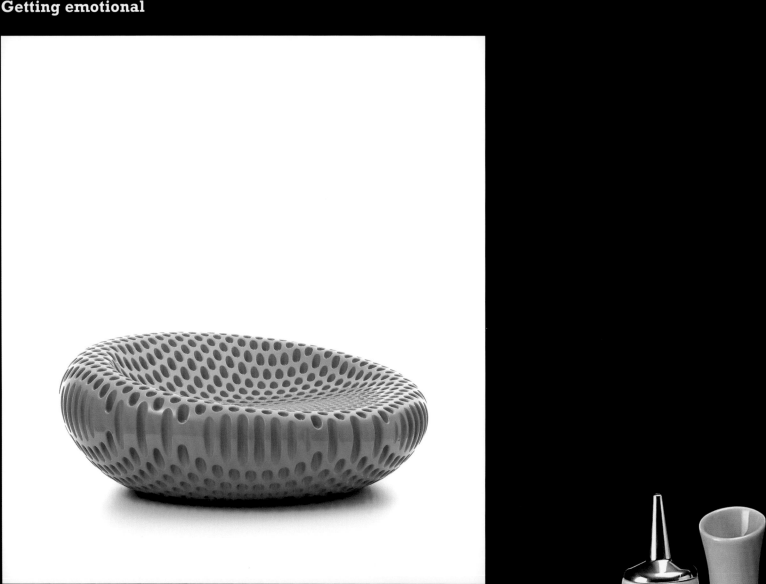

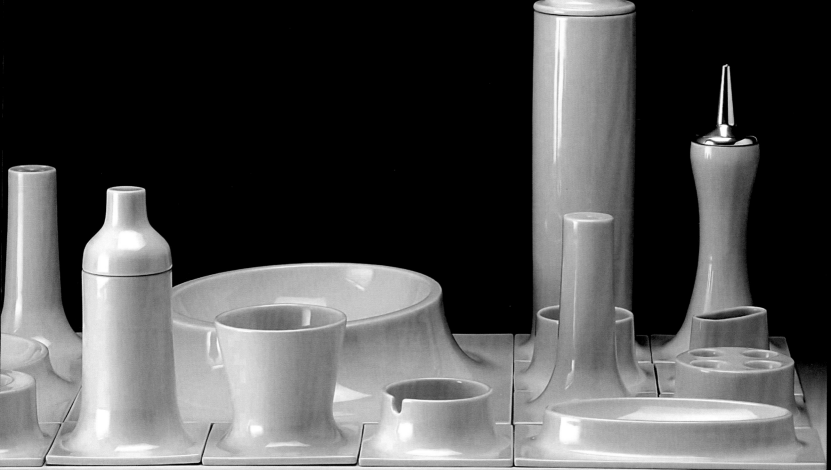

Virtual design

Hack-Mac
Ito Morabito for Ora Ito
France, 1999

Non-commissioned guerrilla designer Ito Morabito created virtual products for companies such as Apple
or Louis Vuitton and placed them as
advertisements in magazines. He
wrapped the spoof Hack-Mac laptop
in bulletproof camouflaged combat
gear, triggering mass hype.

By: Cornelia Haff

Around the World.

Cars may be primarily driving machines, but that tells nothing like the full story. They also represent an expression of lifestyle, a living space, mobile extensions of our homes, the tools of our mobility, high-tech street furniture and places where we work, listen to music and sing without inhibition – to name but a few of their spin-off roles. Cars bring people together, the MINI more so than most. Its success has stretched around the world and melted through barriers of language, culture, latitude and origin. It has become a truly classless, global lifestyle accessory which puts smiles on faces wherever it travels. Ten cult photographers, creative designers and artists from virtually every corner of the earth have showcased the MINI in various contexts: as elements of their world, their city, their styles and their art – a symbol of our society and the times in which we live.

Takashi Homma*
Tokyo
Untitled

* For more information on the artists and
their work, turn to page 48.

Lara Baladi
Cairo
"Would you care for another cup of tea?"

Sune Eriksen
Oslo
"MINI Norway"

Sanchez Brothers
Montreal
''Poutininque Sect of Montréal''

Ümit Ünal
Istanbul
Untitled

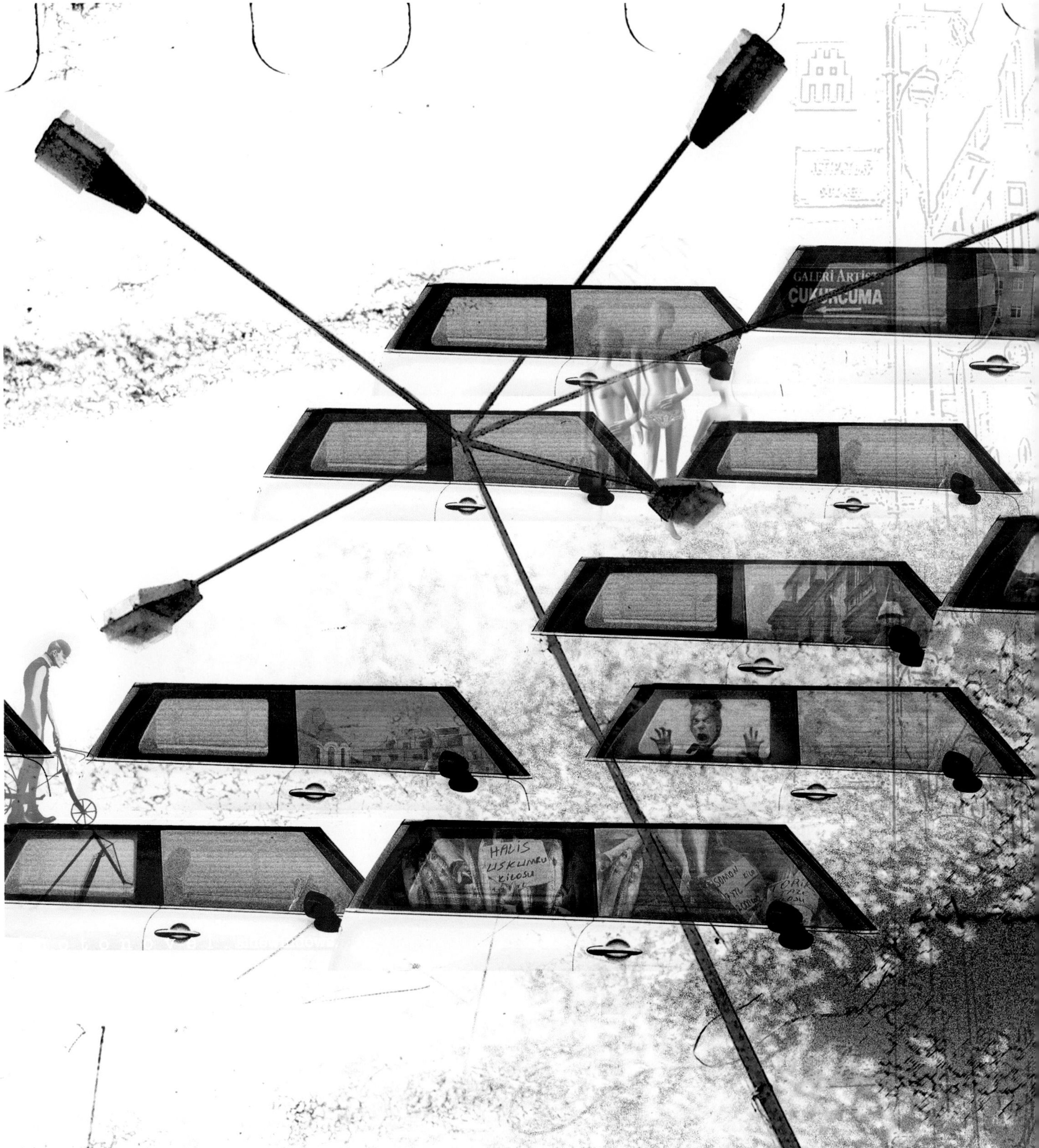

Marcos López
Buenos Aires
"Captain and
Sailors in Buenos
Aires Harbour"

Martin Parr
Bristol
Untitled

Jay FC/China Stylus
Hong Kong
"MINI Hong Kong"

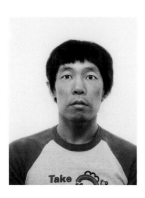

Takashi Homma
Photographer
Tokyo, Japan
p.28

Lara Baladi
Photographer
Cairo, Egypt
p.30

**Gerhard Amstutz /
Franz Rindlisbacher**
Photographers, Zurich, Switzerland
p.32

Sune Eriksen
Photographer
Oslo, Norway
p.34

Takashi Homma is one of Japan's most important contemporary photographers. Born in Tokyo in 1962, Homma has won over the critics with cool, clear and precise images which break free from ideology and focus on everyday scenes – taken in Japanese suburbs, for example. Here, on the outskirts of a city, the fissures in the country's social and economic fabric and the chasm between individual desires and reality are most starkly exposed. Takashi Homma displays a certain lightness of touch in his work – as if the picture is captured in passing. With coolness and attention to detail he tugs at the nerve endings of modern-day society. On an international level, Homma is mentioned in the same breath as star photographers like Andreas Gursky and Jeff Wall. In addition to his artistic work, Homma also contributes to magazines such as *i-D*, *Purple Prose*, *Purple Fashion*, *Switch*, *Elle Deco* (Tokyo), *Ray Gun* and numerous Japanese titles. This untitled image shows Nana and her small brother learning to roller-skate in Shibuya, a district in the heart of Tokyo where small residential houses rub shoulders with skyscrapers. In the background are the Tokyo City Opera Building and the MINI – the perfect car for the world's largest metropolis.

Born in Lebanon in 1969, Lara Baladi lived in Beirut, Paris and London before moving to Cairo, where she has remained since 1997. Her work entitled "Would you care for another cup of tea?" is "a reference to the billboards and posters which litter the roadside all over Egypt", depicting landscapes and scenes that have been visibly computer-enhanced and transformed into blissful idylls featuring objects of desire. Baladi's works have been exhibited in a host of renowned photographic collections, such as the Fondation Cartier in Paris, the Museet for Fotokunst in Copenhagen and the Pori Art Museum in Finland. Most recently, Baladi was one of the artists featured in C on the Cities, part of the Architecture Exhibition at the 2006 Venice Biennale. Baladi's first major solo exhibition Kai'ro was hosted by Sweden's Bildmuseet museum in 2004. Lara Baladi is a member of the Beirut-based Fondation Arabe pour l'Image (FAI), which acts as a guardian of the Arab world's photographic legacy.

41-year-old Gerhard Amstutz from Langenthal in Switzerland – widely known by his photographer alias "gee ly" – and Franz Rindlisbacher, born in 1963, have been working together since 2003. Amstutz started out as a graphic designer and has held Art Director posts for *Das Magazin* and *Annabelle* in Zurich, *German Vogue* in Munich, *swissair gazette* and *Passport*. He has worked as a photographer under his "gee ly" stage name since 2002. Franz Rindlisbacher cut his teeth as a photographer in the worlds of fashion, advertising and architecture. Between 1998 and 2004 he oversaw the fashion faculty at the School of Art and Design Zurich (hgkz). The partnership's "Geschützter Verkehr" (Protected Traffic) series takes the increased use of speed cameras in Zurich as its subject. The cameras now earn the city coffers some 40 million euros per year, provoking wide-ranging local debate. Amstutz/Rindlisbacher capture situations staged in typical Zurich locations from the simultaneous perspective of the speed camera itself and passers-by on the opposite side who hide the MINI number plate from view. This allows them to depict various faces of Zurich while involving the MINI in the debate on the city.
www.gee-ly.ch
www.franzrindlisbacher.ch

Sune Eriksen is a native of the Norwegian capital Oslo and has been working as a photographer since 1991. The 31-year-old made his name through his work for, among others, the prize-winning motoring magazine *Carl's Cars*, and now focuses primarily on travel photography and portraits of musicians. Norway is a small country and the locals have become adept at making maximum use of the space available to them. Eriksen's work "MINI Norway" is set in Hjemmets Kolkonihager, an area dotted with 109 small plots of land each with a house covering no more than 28 square metres. These properties represent a very popular place to spend the summer in Oslo and the waiting list to buy one now stretches for several years. The models used for the photo are Cecilie Roer, a policewoman and car fan, and Martin Staxrud, a sports teacher and surfer. Sune Eriksen's picture offers a brief insight into contemporary Norway, and the photographer sees the MINI as fitting in perfectly with the typical Norwegian scene.

Sanchez Brothers *Photographers* Montreal, Canada p.36	**Ümit Ünal** *Artist and fashion designer* Istanbul, Turkey p.38	**Marcos López** *Photographer* Buenos Aires, Argentina p.40	**Martin Parr** *Photographer* Bristol, England p.42

Now 28 and 24 years old, the Canadian Sanchez Brothers – Carlos and Jason – have earned a reputation as exuberant photographers never short of ideas. They are ranked among the outstanding purveyors of their craft in North America today and are central figures in Montreal's buzzing art scene. Their work is highly coveted by contemporary galleries and they enjoy an enviable reputation among modern photographic art connoisseurs. They are represented by two leading galleries in New York and Toronto. The Sanchez Brothers shoot their pictures like a major Hollywood production. Every detail is planned, the actors are cast, whole sets put together, highly complex lighting set up and nothing left to chance. Their work features snapshots depicting the climax of bizarre, indeed rather surreal stories whose beginning and end are left to the imagination of the beholder. The brothers give "Poutininque Sect of Montréal" an intriguing introduction: "Esteemed audience, ladies and gentlemen, your attention please! Here, before your disbelieving and enraptured rolling eyeballs, you are seeing the inescapable proof that the enchanting and magical Poutininque Sect of Montreal lives on! See how Montreal once was, still is today and will remain forever!" www.thesanchezbrothers.com

Ümit Ünal is one of the most important ambassadors of Istanbul's creative hub. Born in the city straddling the Bosphorus in 1969, he started out studying archaeology and art history in his home town before moving on to textile and fashion design. His studio in an old house on Tünel Square is a wondrous mixture of workshop and stage, a "place of cultural interest" as Ünal himself calls it. An avantgarde antidote to the heady glamour of the fashion scene would also be a fair description – Ümit Ünal is, after all, far more than a fashion designer. He describes how Tünel greets him with a spread of everyday art "totally unaware of its own existence" on his way to work each morning. "Working in a creative field means having your feet grounded in life," says Ünal. "Ultimately, what you're creating is something drawn from life itself. If you know how to live life, it is a source of inspiration." Ünal is not one to rest on his laurels. "The idea of copying something I've already done appals me," he says. Indeed, every exhibition or installation he puts together is a leap into the unknown. Ünal finds his inspiration in books by Camille Claudel, the famous sculptor and lover of Auguste Rodin, and most recently in Karl Valentin, the comedian he admires and who is shown as a bemused observer of the goings on in Ünal's collage of MINI silhouettes. www.umitunal.com

Marcos López was born in 1958 in Santa Fe, Argentina and initially studied engineering before changing tack to photography in 1978. His early work saw him focus on black-and-white documentary-style photos of patients in a neuropsychiatric clinic, and he also worked on projects with various other artists. In 1987 a scholarship took him to Cuba to complete a qualification in video documentary-making. Gabriel García Marquez personally invited López to one of his scriptwriting workshops. It was in Cuba that he discovered the eye-catching colours, carnivalesque vivacity and spontaneity of the Caribbean. His first book, *Retratos* (Photographs, 1993), heralded the dawn of a new era defined as much by realism as by visionary thought: it marked the breakthrough of exuberant colours, ironically staged scenes and an almost unholy socio-critical insight that reinforced his reputation as one of Argentina's most original artists. In his hands, photography becomes the shortest conceivable route between sorrow and happiness, cynicism and compassion, emotions and artificiality, criticism and beauty. Lopez entitled his picture for this book "Captain and Sailors in Buenos Aires Harbour". The MINI in the image is, as he puts it, "a lavish, magnificent diamond in the melancholic city of Buenos Aires". www.marcoslopez.com

Born in Epsom, Surrey in 1952, Martin Parr studied photography at Manchester Polytechnic (as was). He came to the attention of the art world after winning three successive awards from the Arts Council of Great Britain in the late 1970s. Parr's provocative photographic style has sparked heated debate. In 1994 he became a member of the renowned photographic agency Magnum. His pictures have been shown in numerous solo exhibitions worldwide and acquired by major collections of photographic art. Parr has published most of his work in books such as *Bad Weather* (1982), *Bored Couples* (1993) and *Common Sense* (1999). His very British sense of humour shines through in his photographic study of the British lower and middle classes and mass tourism. Among his works as a documentary film-maker are the TV documentary *Think of England*. Parr believes his pictures are self-explanatory and require no interpretation: "I'm a photographer. I don't want to destroy the mystique by taking things apart and analysing them." His quirky image of the MINI parked in front of sloping houses speaks for itself. www.martinparr.com

Olaf Heine
Photographer
Berlin, Germany / Los Angeles, USA
p. 44

Jay FC/China Stylus
Street artist
Hong Kong
p.46

Olaf Heine is one of Germany's most in-demand photographic artists. His work speaks a universal, emotional and in many ways cinematic language, one which is shared on both sides of the Atlantic. Born in Hanover in 1968, Heine first trained as an architectural draughtsman before moving on to study architecture – a background which explains the lines that are found in the majority of his work. One day a musician friend asked him to take some photos of his band, and the rest is history, as they say. Heine photographs artists, actors and musicians. His job is to capture his famous subjects from a new angle, heightening their fame even further. The style of his images is classic, minimalist, aesthetic, and always staged. At the same time, though, he seems to suck the tension out of his photographs. They exude a perfectly relaxed air, like scenes from films which were never actually made. Even the unfussy close-ups of his protagonists send out the scent of a story. Olaf Heine has worked with people like Lou Reed, Iggy Pop, Bon Jovi, Sheryl Crow, Franka Potente, Herbert Grönemeyer, Die Toten Hosen, Radiohead and Coldplay. He leaves it to others to give their thoughts on his work: "It is much more exciting when people with different perspectives describe what they see."
www.olafheine.com

Born in England, self-taught artist Jay FC studied as a marine biologist. His first creative assignments were for a large advertising agency in Hong Kong, where he has worked for twelve years now. In 2000 he founded China Stylus, a creative design studio with a remit to smooth the conflict between creativity and commerce. This was also the motivation behind Jay FC's involvement in ST/ART, a Hong Kong street art initiative, whose ironic and often political works – laced with an overwhelming current of positive energy – crop up frequently in the territory's urban landscape. Together with a selection of other artists around the world, ST/ART has ensured that graffiti is today recognised as a serious form of art. Jay FC's artistic work is "more heavily influenced by what happens around me every day than what other creative people are doing". Hong Kong represents a prime source of inspiration for Jay's work, on both a professional and a personal level. "Chinese graphic design is very influential. My method of working has a lot in common with the ancient Chinese art of paper cutting. My work highlights the vibrancy and contrasts of Hong Kong." And the MINI as a symbol of the city's new era.
www.chinastylus.com
www.start.hk

Paul Smith, Mary Quant, MINI and the Swinging Sixties.

Paul Smith left school at 15, worked as an errand boy in a clothing warehouse and dreamt of becoming a racing cyclist. Pedalling countless miles through his home town of Nottingham, studying coal-miners, Derby tweeds and the elegance of the country squires, he received a head start in matters of style which eventually catapulted him to the pinnacle of world fashion – the only British fashion designer to do so. Paul Smith has a soft spot for British classics, items deeply embedded in the nation's style consciousness, made with meticulous care and of proverbial longevity. These are the products he features in his shops. The Filofax craze of the eighties, for example, was unleashed by Paul Smith, and the boxer shorts cult was of his making as well. Smith's major achievement as a fashion designer are his trademark striped shirts, which have enabled men to display their fashion sense while preserving their masculinity. The MINI is among the British products that Smith has adopted as his own. For a fashion designer with a yearly income well over 200 million pounds, he is surprisingly modest and well-grounded. Apart from his compulsion to collect junk and his extravagant circle of acquaintances (Hanif Kureishi, Sir Terence Conran, David Bowie, Daniel Day-Lewis), the only luxury Smith ever indulges in is a few seconds here and there hovering between heaven and earth: when he balances on his bike in the middle of his office, introducing a brief moment of inertia during his entertaining reflection of the sixties, the MINI and Britishness.

Pinstripes and denim: Paul Smith goes for relaxed mode, whether in fashion, art or his designer armchair.

Where it all began: Paul Smith, future king of the striped look, plays the tailor's dummy in his very first shop.

55

He may have his own *parking spot in London for his MINI, but Paul Smith still occasionally takes his bike to the office.*

Paul Smith helped men to discover fashion for themselves: they were made to feel stylish and masculine not just in dark suits but equally in mega-checks, pop outfits and patent leather overknees.

What've you got in your pockets? Unusually for me, nothing. What, no toys or gadgets? Nope. Sorry, just emptied them. But there's plenty of junk to play with in my office if you want – look, here you go. How do you decide what's junk and what might come in useful for a new creation? I've no idea, we've been doing things this way for years. You know, you take a white shirt, then give it a tweak. No more than a tweak, mind. Just enough of a tweak is all it takes. The same applies to life in general. And what direction do you tweak it in? We just let it roll. The destinations are always the same – work, home, work, home. What radio station do you listen to in the morning? Destination Anywhere? I like listening to Motown on Smooth FM or the news on Radio 4. What does the chauffeur think of that? I'm my own chauffeur. I've had this black MINI for three years now and I drive it to work every morning. I'm allowed to park it on a tiny patch of concrete at the end of the road. My own parking space in London, now how cool is that! It kind of suits you that you drive a MINI, but isn't the new version a bit too, shall we say, corporate for your tastes? No way! I love it. I do in fact have an old 1955 Bristol 405 in the garage. I even brought it out recently for a photo shoot. But to be honest I'm thinking of selling it because I drive it so rarely these days. How come you haven't got one of the limited-edition MINI Classic you helped design? I have. I keep it in Italy, near Florence. A blue one. The same colour as that legendary shirt you wowed the public with at the car's launch in 1998? Exactly. Can you remember the first time you drove from your home in Nottingham to London? Of course. It was in an ancient Morris Minor I'd been given for my 18th birthday. There was an old transistor radio in the boot. It took us over four hours to get there – nowadays you can do it in about 50 minutes. We usually aimed to arrive in London on a Friday night or Saturday afternoon so we could listen to the bands. I used to sleep on a mate's floor in a kind of squat in Porchester Terrace, Notting Hill. Not that we slept much in those days. So from your hangout in that famous little pub in Nottingham, how did you experience the cultural explosion that took place in the sixties? I get worried when I catch myself coming over all nostalgic for the sixties. I think teenagers from every generation have a fantastic time – falling in love for the first time, having sex for the first time, listening to music. On the other hand, the sixties were really something special – life just wouldn't have been the same without them. Why not? The sixties were a catalyst. After the horrors of the war and the poverty and deprivations of the post-war years, it was the first time a generation could really sit back and relax. What happened was seismic, with new ideas sprouting all over the place – in architecture, in music, in graphic design... The MINI Classic was a product of necessity. In the aftermath of the Suez crisis people were looking for something that was economical on fuel and yet suited a family of four... Sure, it had to be absolutely practical. But it was also fast, sexy and innovative. I was a massive fan because the original design was also really functional. There were more and more cars on the roads, and everyone seemed to be going somewhere in a hurry. The times were starting to move more quickly – and the days when you could park in front of your own house were long gone? It was also a really simple design. It hadn't been done before. Did you have friends who owned a MINI Classic? Yeah, one of them had a Mini Van. You could lie down in the back – that was amazing. Was the MINI Classic a cool car to be seen in? You bet. And good for amorous adventures? Sure it was. Ten times better than any of those enormous American imports – much cosier! How did the MINI Classic come to be as much an icon as the Union Jack and the Beatles? I'm not sure. Perhaps through its association with films like *The Italian Job*. Concorde, the London Underground map and red telephone boxes. It took a while, but MINI Classic were extremely sexy, especially once they began competing in rallies. People started sticking go-faster stripes down the side panels – you know, black and white diamonds or whatever they felt like. Things are a bit different nowadays in the automotive industry, what with all the safety aspects to observe... Yes, it's sad to say, but design is a lot more complicated with all the

Made for each other: Paul Smith and the MINI Classic. Shown here, his own blue model from the limited edition he designed himself in 1998.

Side by side through the swinging sixties: Paul Smith was friends with Pink Floyd during London's heyday. Who would have guessed that such promising futures lay in store for all of them?

Give peace a chance: Eric Clapton and his girlfriend, caught up in the spirit of the times.

Centre of a parallel universe: Carnaby Street became the symbol of swinging London in the sixties.

Best of British: sporting the colours of the Union Jack, a late sixties MINI Classic poses in front of Tower Bridge.

Part of the mod movement, The Who emerged as one of Britain's leading rock bands with albums like "Tommy" and "Quadrophenia".

Unmistakably Paul Smith: nobody mixes multicoloured stripes with the same panache – even on a 1997 MINI Classic.

New out of old: in his 2006 autumn/winter collection, Paul Smith experiments with patterns usually found in aging tapestries.

Inspired by MINI: this stylish handbag is a perfect blend of MINI and Paul Smith.

tedious rules and regulations. You are a very keen cyclist, yet you still have a great affection for cars. You also sell vacuum cleaners in your shops. Is the importance we increasingly attach to the design of household objects excessive or justified? More than justified. After all, these objects are what define our daily lives. Take wheelchairs, for example. Until five years ago they looked like hospital rejects. But today a wheelchair can look as good as a Porsche. Or imagine you had to open a bottle without the use of your hands. Design can significantly improve the quality of life for disabled people. Were you concerned that BMW might focus so much on practical features they would fail to capture the charm of MINI Classic? No, I think they've captured that well. They've succeeded in making the MINI sexy for anyone who wants to find it sexy, and non-existent for those who couldn't care less. Even though it's fast and manoeuvrable, the MINI remains pretty unobtrusive. There are parallels here to Paul Smith Enterprises: we're a large company and yet we remain light on our feet, quick, nimble yet always... ...grounded? Like the MINI. Lightweight and lightning quick. You could easily have sold your business years ago to one of the mega-companies queuing at your door. Was this modesty – which could also be a kind of vanity – part of the concept from the outset? No, of course not. It's what carries you through the different trends and fashion movements that would otherwise give you the jitters. In the 1990s, when Gucci and other big labels were taken over by the giants, when everyone was developing innovative store concepts and advertising strategies, and when people were pumping stacks of money into marketing and publicity, I began to feel very insecure. I began thinking perhaps my shops look too old-fashioned, perhaps I should sell up, perhaps I ought to own more stores. Then luckily something – I've no idea what – made me realise that doing things my way was pretty unique. That I didn't necessarily have to change, because Paul Smith was a bit different and able to keep going in its own friendly way. Did you like the fact that you were always seen as being rather different from other fashion designers? In the early years it was very difficult to be taken seriously by the so-called elite magazines and stylists if they couldn't pigeonhole you. In fact it's still the same today – they don't know where to place you if you're not a snob, not pretentious, not full of ego, if you don't go to the right openings, to the shows, the exhibitions and parties. What's happened to your ego these days? You don't need one. All you need is a bit of peace to get on with what you're doing. That's another pretty exceptional quality – the way you stand up for tradition and yet always manage somehow to create something new, without a hint of self-righteousness. You take something old and throw it back into the general lifecycle. Do you do that out of a sense of respect? Out of a sense of fun. I like playing with these objects – hard and soft, kitchen and glamour, tradition and fun, good taste and bad taste. The most important thing is that it looks good. That's just the way I am. I've no idea if that's a good way of working or not. The rest of the world refers to this natural charm as Cool Britannia and wonders why it doesn't work anywhere else... We British tend not to spend so much time worrying about it. All you've got to do is observe. That's how I started. I didn't have much choice in the matter when I was working as an errand boy in a warehouse at the age of 15. I watched how everything was done. Then I ordered fabrics, packed clothes, worked in sales, made designs, decorated windows. I opened shops, managed them, and the whole time I was watching how people got on with one another. Your favourite topic again – communication. That's it. You run a tiny shop and a customer comes in. What do you do to make him come back again? Maybe you can't afford to buy in new clothes two weeks later, but at least you can hang up a picture, paint the wall green, engage him in conversation. One reason that Paul Smith has been so unbelievably successful in Japan was that you didn't just fly out there on a junket. On the contrary. I was so excited to be invited there in the 1980s that I asked if I could bring along my wife Pauline, who was then my girlfriend. We both flew economy class and couldn't believe we were actual-

Whoever said stripes always have to be vertical? In autumn and winter 2006, Paul Smith takes a sideways slant with thick horizontal stripes.

A not-so-wild take on the sixties: fashion designer John Stephen, aka the "King of Carnaby Street", outside his shop with his posh motor.

Skirt and car are cut equally short and colours are *bold*. Black saloons are for the rest. Want to be cutting edge? Stick to MINI Classic.

London in the sixties: Chippendale and Chesterfield may have given way to rock music and miniskirts, but patriotism and the *Union Jack* were always in style.

Despite its endless variety, the famed sixties look was established by a select few. In the vanguard was *Mary Quant*, whose shiny, head-to-toe leather outfits took aback the establishment.

Glory days: with the Beatles topping the charts and London turning into the capital of worldwide *youth*, Paul Smith ventured down from Nottingham.

The wild, raucous Rolling Stones were a perfect counterpoint to the smart mop-top Beatles. It was a long time before the general public could truly comprehend the scale of the cultural *revolution* happening in their midst.

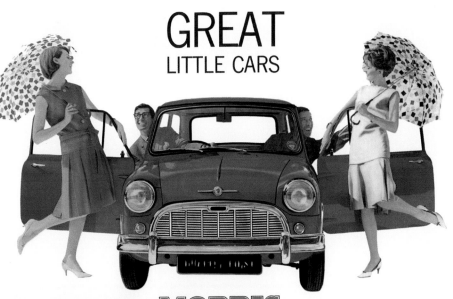

GREAT
LITTLE CARS

MORRIS
MINI-MINORS

A vehicle as unique as its time: originally conceived as a practical, thrifty family car, the Morris Mini quickly turned into a treasured, *glamorous* car for the in-crowd.

Portobello Market: the hub of alternative subculture in sixties London.

Engaged to famed photographer David Bailey and one of the very first supermodels, Jean Shrimpton was also the first to wear a type of mini in 1965, grabbing the world's attention.

ly getting to discover this place called Japan. There were lots of fashion people there, most of whom complained the whole time that nobody spoke English. But to me that's the most fascinating aspect. I've got about 600 employees here in London, 40 in France, 40 in Italy and loads and loads in Japan. It fascinates me to see how they talk, how they work, what they want, why some are more aggressive, others quieter or more easily upset. Is that why you refused to take a private jet? Yes, because there's nothing to see otherwise. It's wonderful to have the chance to observe people, to go to restaurants where you don't know anybody, to sit in traffic jams by yourself, to have people around you other than those you employ. If you don't, you quickly lose the plot. It's all about close observation. William Gibson claims that a key success factor in the development of contemporary fashion design was the Houndsditch fleamarket, a sort of Dickensian institution established over 150 years ago in south London, where dealers took old items of clothing apart and stitched them back together again for resale. Is that why you go to Portobello Market every week? It's true I've been going there almost every weekend throughout my entire life. I live just round the corner. I walk the full length of the market and nearly always find something I can learn from. Sometimes one gets the feeling of having come across your items of clothing before, so that you feel almost a bit uneasy at first, then after a while they become a part of you. That's precisely my point, that's what I'm about. I love it when I meet people on the street and they show me where their shirt is fraying at the edges and say that's why they're so attached to it. Then I know it's an extension of my personality. But I've never really analysed it. You go to a top design label and it's all to do with how powerful and influential you want to appear, how much attention you want to draw to yourself, how chic and sexy everything is. You owe this down-to-earth quality to your wife Pauline, who at the age of 21 showed you how to sew on a sleeve. I was often pretty wild with Pauline, drunk a lot of the time. Loads of my friends were musicians – Led Zeppelin, Pink Floyd, Eric Clapton.

Pauline calmed me down a bit. We met on my 21st birthday and since then we've done everything together. Is it true you don't have a computer at home, no mobile phones and not even an answering machine? Doesn't that make it even harder to invite you to the parties you rarely turn up at these days? Pauline likes writing letters. And this new striped iMac here in your office? That's a present from the Apple designer Jonathan Ive, another good friend of mine. A colleague uses it. It's all a mystery to me. And yet you are pretty much at one with yourself. What's the secret to your long and happy marriage? Finding the right balance. Between giving and taking. Understanding what the other person needs. Being interested. And I suppose a bit of love doesn't come amiss.

Interview: Kristin Rübesamen

Paul Smith – brief biography

1946	*Born in Nottingham*
1961	*Leaves school without any qualifications, begins job in a clothing warehouse*
1963	*Serious cycling accident, spends three months in hospital. Begins ordering menswear for the department store*
1964	*Works as a manager in a girlfriend's store*
1967	*Moves out of parents' house and in with girlfriend Pauline Denyer*
1970	*Opens first shop in Nottingham – Vêtement Pour Homme – measuring 16 square metres*
1976	*First Paris show of his own collection*
1979	*Opens first London shop in Floral Street, begins selling Filofaxes*
1982	*Opens second shop in Avery Row*
1984	*Initiates Japanese business venture with Itochu*
1987	*Opens first shop in Manhattan, in the West Village*
1994	*Presents his first women's collection*
1995	*Wins Queen's Award for Export. "Paul Smith True Brit" exhibition opens in London's Design Museum*
1997	*Invited by the British government to participate in a creative task force*
1998	*Launch of the limited-edition Paul Smith MINI Classic*
2001	*Knighthood from the Queen, marries Pauline Denyer*

www.paulsmith.co.uk

In the sixties, Paul Smith set out to make his mark on the style of a new era. Meanwhile, girlfriend and eventual wife Pauline Denyer made sure he did not venture too far onto the wild side.

Rock band Led Zeppelin brought a completely new world of sound to popular music.

Mary Quant: the woman with the trademark black bob is a classic example of how fashion is often the harbinger of sweeping social developments. In the mid-fifties, Mary Quant was already thinking, living and designing what would come to define the sixties: liberated women flouting convention, the younger generation in the vanguard, and fashion as a medium. "It is given to a fortunate few to be born at the right time, in the right place, with the right talents. In recent fashion there are three: Chanel, Dior and Mary Quant" wrote a *Sunday Times* fashion editor. Quant was born in 1934, the daughter of a Welsh schoolteacher. She studied fashion illustration at London's Goldsmiths College and went on to work for a milliner. It was here that she discovered she did not want to cater to a select minority who could afford to buy haute couture, but would rather focus her efforts towards a new, upcoming generation – those who would go on to shape the sixties as groovy, fashion-conscious mods in London or as student activists in Paris and Berlin clamouring for political change.

In 1959 Quant invented the revolutionary miniskirt that ended some way above the knee. Every woman wanted to wear it and every man wanted to see them in it. It is a commonly held belief that it was named after the diminutive car favoured by the young set who shopped in Quant's boutique "Bazaar" in Chelsea and, like her, beat a trail to a certain Vidal Sassoon for their haircuts. It was for this "Chelsea Set" that Quant began designing fashions which her youthful clientele could afford to buy, long before Yves Saint Laurent came up with Pret à Porter. With her teen look – miniskirts, PVC coats, snug-fitting ribbed sweaters – she ushered in the decline of Christian Dior's New Look, which had previously ruled the fashion roost. Mary Quant remains a successful figure in the fashion scene to this day, primarily through her cosmetics lines. Japan has more than 200 stores displaying her logo, a stylised, almost childlike image of a daisy – a symbol of the swinging sixties.

London 1967: Mary Quant practises what she preaches. Her trademark is the miniskirt.

Mary Quant on everyday life:
I don't really have a normal day. Every day is different as I work on different things. I work for the House of Fraser, I study fashion in the stores at retail and the exclusive fashion boutiques in Sloane Street and Bond Street and in Paris. I see many of the student graduate collections in London. I write occasional pieces for newspapers and magazines, give talks at some of the fashion design schools, answer questions from journalists and cook Italian food. A perfect weekend is one spent in my farmhouse in France, in my garden in England, at the Colombe d'Or hotel in St. Paul de Vence or at the Bulgari in Milan.

Classics of the post-war era were presented at the exhibition "From the Bomb to the Beatles" in the Imperial War Museum. Among them, the very first *MINI Classic* and models wearing *Mary Quant's miniskirts and dresses.*

...on today's fashions:

I am fascinated by Chloé, Chanel, Conran and some of the new young student graduates in fashion right now. The fact that fashion is so celebrity-driven these days makes it more individual and not limited to the styles that only top international models can wear. It keeps fashion young and zesty. My prediction is that vulgarity will become the new elegance. The new and original is often described as vulgar by people who haven't caught up with it yet. Vulgarity is life. Good taste is death.

Mary Quant's fashions put their stamp on "Swinging London"; her dresses became *icons of the sixties.*

The fashion designer working in her London studio *in October 1967.*

Revival of two sixties stars: in 1988 Mary Quant customised a limited-edition MINI Classic with black and white striped seats in op-art look.

The Beatles and the MINI Classic seemed to be kindred spirits: Ringo Starr with a 1964 Rallye Monte Carlo Mini Cooper.

...on cars:

I love the new MINI. It's a stylish, happy, smiling car. My first car was a MINI Classic – black with black leather seats. I bought it and paid for it – a special order. But my husband Alexander Plunkett Greene changed the order to an automatic gearbox without telling me because I had only just passed my driving test. I was furious. I had learnt to drive on Alexander's E-type Jaguar, which scared the living daylights out of him and me. But as a result I have never been able to go back to a shift gearbox – so he was right. With the MINI Classic I felt totally free and emancipated because with a tank full of petrol one could go anywhere and one had a mobile roof over one's head. With those bucket door pockets there was room for a pair of boots, a bottle of wine, a toothbrush, a ham sandwich and a bathing suit. It was so neat and easy to drive and park, and the seats and windows and mirrors were just right. I also customised a MINI Classic. You could have a black, white or silver MINI Classic with black and white bold striped seats and a Mary Quant daisy badge. I don't know how many were made. Some probably still exist.

Short, sharp, sassy: the *Mary Quant look* was unmistakable.

…on the sixties:

My style of fashion made women look like a younger version of themselves, like a girl. It added a playful teenage quality to them, a great mix between innocence and sexiness. These women always looked curious, they explored the world, defied the rules and defined their own new standards. I certainly wanted to achieve a young, new, sexy chic which defined its own route. As does the MINI Classic. The sixties was the best ten-year party ever. The best legacy of the Chelsea set is Chelsea itself. Chelsea is the best village in London. The parking the worst.

In 1967 Quant (centre) had already taken up *shoe design* – and the fashion world lay at her feet.

And now for the *men:* in 1972 Mary Quant fastens one of her ties around the neck of TV host Michael Parkinson.

70

Skinny supermodel in a minidress, 1966: Twiggy redefined the ideal of beauty for a whole generation.

The designer and "her" model conquer the fashion world: Mary Quant and Twiggy on the cover of "Vogue".

VOGUE

REUSSIR VOTRE ETE A COUP SUR

EN ROBES DE COTON ET D'ORGANDI EN MAILLOTS SHORTS ET EN BLAZERS

…on the relationship between cars and fashion: The MINI Classic influenced the fashion industry, it perfectly fitted the new young career girl. It still makes a fashion statement and is a favourite here and in Paris. No one seems to know whether the name MINI was invented for the car or the skirt. I did meet Issigonis but I was so overwhelmed I didn't dare ask him.

Never before was there so much leg about: the perfect accessories for Mary Quant's minidress were green net stockings and Charles Jourdan court shoes – budget permitting.

The typical Quant look in 1967: the "Banana Split" with high collar and long zip in contrasting colour.

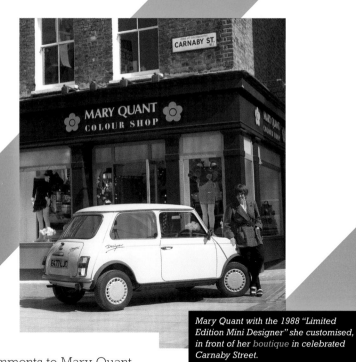

Mary Quant with the 1988 "Limited Edition Mini Designer" she customised, in front of her boutique in celebrated Carnaby Street.

…on Japan:

I send ideas and comments to Mary Quant Japan – study fabrics and colours. The Japanese take immense trouble about detail when making things beautifully. Japanese girls wear Mary Quant fashion so well and use Mary Quant make-up with a perfect chic simplicity. Japanese girls are very beautiful.

Brief biography of Mary Quant:

1934	Born in London
1955	Opens the first boutique in Chelsea with her future husband Alexander Plunkett Greene
1962	Starts an eleven-year collaboration as a designer for JC Penney
1963	Mary Quant Ginger Group set up
1963	Receives Sunday Times International Award
1966	Mary Quant cosmetics line launched
1966	Autobiography "Quant by Quant" published
1966	Made an OBE
1969	Named Royal Designer for Industry
1973	"Mary Quant's London" exhibition in the London Museum, Kensington Palace
1983	Mary Quant fashion and cosmetics launched in Japan; first Colour Shop opens in Japan
1984	Publication of "Colour by Quant"
1986	Publication of "Quant on Make-Up"
1994	Mary Quant Colour Shop opens in Chelsea; further shops in Paris and Knightsbridge follow
1998	First Mary Quant Concept Shop opens on New York's Madison Avenue

www.maryquant.co.uk

Model Peggy Moffit in a 1967 seer-sucker dress with gathered waist.

The
Legends.

The MINI Classic is a symbol of the 20th century, a landmark piece of design and a technical revolution. Its history is closely intertwined with the lives of three men who made an extraordinary car into an icon: Sir Alec Issigonis, the legendary designer and brains behind the MINI Classic, John Cooper, who turned it into a hot-heeled racer, and Rauno Aaltonen, the "Flying Finn" who won more major races in the MINI Classic than any other driver. These are the stories of three heroes of the automotive world.

Alec Issigonis

—

The mastermind

A greek born in present-day turkey designed a car in England that went on to conquer the world: The designer of the MINI Classic was a man who thought out of the box. He single-handedly dreamed up the car's revolutionary basic design and in so doing wrote automotive history.

— By Mark van Huisseling

— There are those who turn for inspiration to management books and self-help aids that subscribe to the "crisis as opportunity" approach to life. And you wonder. But the career of Alec Issigonis is proof of the fact that "crisis as opportunity" really can be more than just a cliché. Sir Alec Issigonis was born Alexander Arnold Constantine Issigonis in Izmir on February 18th, 1906. In those days the Aegean coastal town was known as Smyrna. It was not a peaceful place, nor were these peaceful times. Alexander was just twelve when the first shots were exchanged in the war between Greece and Turkey, and when Turkish soldiers conquered Smyrna, he and his parents – father Greek, mother from Württemberg in southern Germany – fled by ship to England. His father died before they arrived there.

As a boy growing up in Smyrna, Alexander had once been given a ride in a Cadillac. Aged 18 and now settled in London, he adopted the name Alec, and was presented with his first car as a gift from his mother. It was a Singer with a Weymann body. Prior to this, though, the boy had shown no particular interest in vehicles and no signs that one day he would be hailed – in the opinion of Ulf Poschardt, motoring correspondent for the Swiss weekly *Schweizer Weltwoche* and author of the book *Über Sportwagen* – as one of the world's "top three automotive designers – along with Henry Ford and Ferdinand Alexander Porsche".

In 1925, now aged 19, Alec Issigonis applied for a place to study engineering science at Battersea Polytechnic in London. Surprisingly, perhaps, the man who would later dream up one of the most ingenious and complete examples of automotive design did not originally train as a designer but as an engineer. "That may well account for why his designs were so revolutionary," says Alfredo Häberli, a designer who numbers Volvo among his clients. "As an engineer he approached problem-solving from a different angle." In fact, to be strictly accurate, having failed his final examinations Mr Issigonis was not actually entitled to call himself a qualified engineer. According to Alice Rawsthorn, the former director of the Design Museum in London, while his drawing work was considered "excellent", he failed mathematics at three successive attempts.

But as Mick Jagger and Bill Gates can testify, those who abandon their studies or flunk their finals are often more successful in real life than those who graduate with top honours.

In any case, it appears Issigonis' inability to calculate was due in large part to a sizeable lack of interest. Throughout his professional career he never concerned himself much with figures and had little time for the "bean counters" at the companies he worked for. As the examiners at Battersea Polytechnic discovered, his talent was for drawing. But more than that, in just a few swift strokes on paper Issigonis had the ability to realise visions – here, for once, the word can be used in its truest sense. It didn't even have to be paper. Legend has it that the preliminary sketch for the MINI Classic, which originally answered to the names Austin Seven or Morris Mini-Minor, was made on a napkin while sipping gin on a hotel terrace at Cannes on the Côte d'Azur. "A very civilised approach to development," noted James Dyson, designer of the revolutionary bagless vacuum cleaner that bears his name, in an interview for CNN.

The legend would even have us believe that the French hotel's square of linen bearing Issigonis' sketch underwent no significant modifications and actually served as the template from which the designers derived the plans that lay behind the 5,387,862 MINI Classic models built between 1959 and 2000. In any case, what was there to change? The groundbreaking idea that made the diminutive model possible was already contained in the original drawing, namely the mounting of the engine "side-to-side" as opposed to "front-to-back" above the front axle. This was what made it possible to shorten the bonnet and devote 80 percent of the three-metre body to the benefit of driver and passengers. The legendary napkin with the original drawing has meanwhile become the Turin Shroud of the design world. "I searched high and low to find a copy I could take to customers and show them what it means to come up with the 'surprise solution'," says designer Häberli.

Returning briefly to the subject of "crisis as opportunity", the fact that Issigonis got the job at all was in fact the result of a real-life crisis. When the President of Egypt, Gamal Abd el Nasser, closed the Suez Canal in 1956, Great Britain found itself in an oil crisis. That was the cue for bosses at the British Motor Corporation (BMC) – the company that resulted from the merger between Morris Motors and the Austin Motor Company – to ask Issigonis to develop a fuel-efficient four-seater vehicle. A few years earlier he had been commissioned to design an 8-cylinder sports saloon for the smaller manufacturer Alvis. Given Issigonis' antipathy towards luxury – on four wheels at least – it was in many ways rather strange that he should have taken on such a job, although he is on record as having once said, "I would like people to sit on nails – to be extremely uncomfortable all the time." Alec Issigonis, who was

Right and below: Sir Alec Issigonis at his desk in Longbridge and with the Morris Mini-Minor No. 1 at his retirement in 1971.

Left: Why not mount the engine transversely to save space? Issigonis' creativity was boundless. With the MINI Classic he hit the jackpot.

Below: Always a better draughtsman than mathematician – Alec Issigonis at the drawing board.

awarded a knighthood in 1969, was not always the easiest person to work with, it seems. In an interview published in the magazine *Autocar* on August 25th, 1979, the picture that emerges is of someone who was eccentric and engaging by turn and, on occasion, even came across as uncouth or condescending.

The journalist asked what he would be doing on August 26th to celebrate the 20th anniversary of the MINI Classic. "I'll be going to a restaurant not far from my home in Edgbaston, because I can't stand restaurants I don't know." – "Let's talk about cars; after all that's why I'm here – the Morris Minor, the MINI Classic, the 1100, the 1800..." – "How dull, my dear." – "Very well, what are you most proud of?" enquired the questioner in a vain attempt to rescue her interview. "To have been made a member of the Royal Society and to have my name entered into the book alongside Charles II and James Watt."

Although Sir Alec spent the greater part of his working life as a salaried employee, he was certainly no company man – at least not the sort the human resources manager of a major company would look for today. "Fiercely independent and proud of being uncompromising" is how Alice Rawsthorn from the Design Museum describes him. He regarded market analysis as "bunk" and called mathematics "the enemy of every truly creative mind". It would certainly not have been easy in the 1950s for

someone so utterly independent and proud of his uncompromising nature to get his ideas accepted by a capital-intensive industry that risked losing billions of pounds and thousands of jobs if an idea flopped.

And yet with his revolutionary ideas, Sir Alec managed to deliver results that the bean counters he so despised could never have predicted. "He was a genius, the mastermind who anticipated everything we now see in contemporary small-car design," says author Ulf Poschardt. "His whole approach to work – designing a car more or less single-handedly – would be impossible today." For Alfredo Häberli, on the other hand, such independence is key: "'There have got to be people like Issigonis today. Without developers who are able to think differently there can be no development."

Sir Alec, who died in 1988, would probably have subscribed to that. "The most important thing I have learned," he once said, "is that when designing a new car for production, never, never copy the competition." It's a satisfying "Issigonism" on which to end. But for Sir Alec Issigonis, the sentiment is somehow much too conciliatory. More fitting, perhaps, to finish with something more representative of the great man: "I hate everything that's big – big houses, big companies and more than anything, big cars."

Below: Ingenious design. The wheels of the 1958 prototype were positioned at the car's four corners, leaving 80 percent of its three-metre length for the benefit of passengers.

Bottom: Miracle of space. The Morris Mini-Minor of 1959 in longitudinal cutaway. The three suitcases in the boot must also have been in mini-format.

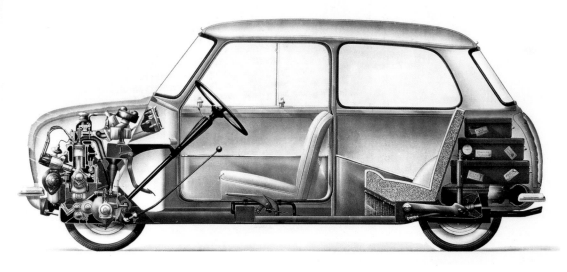

John Cooper

—

The kingmaker

Almost from birth, John Cooper had eyes for one thing above all else: racing cars – and the faster the better. The brilliant engine developer gave the MINI Classic an extra dynamic spark, creating a racing car brimming with glamour and dash.

— By Sebastian Hammelehle

Reims, 1958: the eve of the Formula One race at the French circuit. In a typically unpretentious scene from the world of 1950s motor sport, the drivers had gathered in a bar for a pre-race tipple. Having put away a tidy amount of the landlord's finest, they placed bets on who could climb one of the trees outside the fastest. Intrigued by the noise and laughter, Stirling Moss walked out of the bar to find something dripping on his head from above. Moss looked up and saw a chortling Mike Hawthorn. Having climbed the tree, Hawthorn suddenly needed to take a leak and wasn't going to make it to the gents in time. The only option was to relieve himself from the top of the tree – onto the head of his compatriot and rival. Hawthorn drove his Ferrari to victory in the race the following day and ended the season as world champion. For Moss, who went on to become the most famous of all British racing drivers, defeat on the track made it a weekend to forget.

John Cooper was one of those at the bar that evening and there was great amusement when he recounted the story a number of years later. Cooper loved Formula One, loved cars and loved just having fun. The dark-haired Briton with the striking eyebrows and straw hat refuelled the team's cars himself with a jerry can and funnel. And when one of his drivers won a race, he would celebrate with a trademark somersault – out on the race track.

The year after that night in Reims it was a driver from Cooper's team who was crowned world champion: Jack Brabham. The real sensation, however, was not the Cooper team's maiden success, but Brabham's car. The Cooper Climax was painted in traditional British racing green, resembled a baguette sandwich on wheels, and was the first successful mid-engined car in Formula One. Cooper preferred to breeze over his innovation with classic British understatement: "We mounted the engine further back for the simple reason that it was more practical to do so."

But that disguises the truly groundbreaking nature of Cooper's idea. Today, all Formula One cars have the engine mounted near the centre of the car and Cooper has gone on to become a legendary figure. The public at large, however, know him better as the man who – for four decades now – has given his name to upgraded versions of a very different type of car: the MINI.

Just the name of race team owner Cooper was enough to earn the MINI Classic – launched with moderate success as an economical petrol-engined car in 1959 – an enviable glamour and secure it the big breakthrough in the early 1960s. Cooper turned the journey from England to the Italian Grand Prix into a full-blooded race with an Aston Martin, his tuned MINI Classic arriving in Monza over an hour ahead of the larger car.

Cooper had already known Alec Issigonis for a number of years, and even competed against the inventor of the MINI Classic in a hill-climb event. Eventually he also convinced the British Motor Corporation, which was building the MINI Classic at the time, to bring a version with more horsepower and higher speed onto the market. That car was the Mini Cooper.

It was only with the sprinkling of motor sport's stardust that the MINI Classic became the iconic British car of the 1960s. Everybody from aristocrats like Lord Snowdon, the Queen's former brother-in-law, to actor Peter Sellers, Ringo Starr of Beatles fame and Twiggy, the original stick-thin supermodel, were seen at the wheel. The MINI Classic became a figurehead for "Swinging London".

John Cooper himself had little time for pop music and the euphoria whipped up during the sixties. "He was only concerned with one thing: motor sport, motor sport, motor sport," remembers his son Michael.

Cooper set up his workshop in Surbiton, southwest London. Eric Clapton went to school in the same area and used to pop by to chat with the mechanics in the afternoons. In subsequent years, Clapton and his schoolfriend Jeff Beck were on the guest list for teeny parties hosted by Cooper's daughter. Once, in the late sixties, Michael had to clear out his hobby room so that a certain actor could stay over. Steve McQueen was coming to visit during a course of driving lessons with John Cooper in preparation for his up-coming motor racing film Le Mans.

Born in 1923, John Cooper competed in his first race at the age of twelve in a racing car built by his father Charles Cooper, a motor sport mechanic by trade. He'd completed no more than a few laps when the race steward spotted him and sent him packing with the message "You're still far too young, lad!" ringing in his ears.

"He was a speed fanatic," recalls Michael Cooper of his father, who left school at 15 to start work at his father's (Michael's grandfather's) workshop. From 1948 he built racing cars at his modest premises near London, one of which was bought by future Formula One impresario Bernie Ecclestone.

The Cooper Car Company refused to be tempted into rampant expansion; indeed, there were never more than 25 mechanics beavering away in the team's small garage – even during its world championship winning pomp.

In those days, Formula One was nothing like the billion-dollar business it is now. An employee later recounted how Cooper allowed the team members expenses of three pounds per day for the trip to Monte

Right: At weekends, the small car was transformed into a racing machine. Here Mini Coopers race at Silverstone in 1965.

Below: Searching for that bit extra... John Cooper in 1958 at the wheel of one of the first Morris Mini-Minors.

Carlo for the Monaco Grand Prix. The lion's share of the race prize "money" was made up of champagne, with the fastest driver in practice for the GP in Reims handed a hundred bottles of bubbly for his efforts. Cooper used every trick in the book to get his hands on it and regularly passed through British customs with a suspiciously large number of cases and boxes – all filled with champagne.

In time, Cooper's racing activities also involved the MINI Classic, and a highly tuned Mini Cooper roared to victory in the Rallye Monte Carlo in 1964, 1965 and 1967. The legendary red car with the white roof, white bonnet stripes and two auxiliary headlamps has since taken on an iconic status worthy of immortalisation in an Andy Warhol pop-art print.

Wonderful anecdotes abound. One hot English summer's day during preparations for the race in Monte Carlo, for example, Cooper was so gripped by watching Paddy Hopkirk in action that he set the race steward's tower alight with a thoughtlessly discarded cigar.

To take the acceleration of the MINI Classic to the next level, Cooper began work on a twin-engined model. However, during testing in London the tyre synchronisation failed, the car rolled over several times and Cooper was thrown out of the car – shortly before it exploded. It was a crash he only narrowly survived and it necessitated a period of recuperation. He spent the time in Sussex and kept himself busy by preparing the ground for and completing the purchase of a car workshop and showroom in the area. The race team owner had become a car dealer. As for the cars in Cooper's private garage, there was a Rolls-Royce – and a MINI Classic. And every time a customer expressed an interest in buying the MINI Classic owned personally by the famous John Cooper, the shrewd businessman simply arranged the sale.

"He always said 'If you go into motor sport, make sure you're spending somebody else's money'," says Michael Cooper, recalling some fatherly advice. Indeed, John Cooper bade farewell to the racing scene when the business of running a team started to get seriously expensive in the late 1960s. Not long after, the new owners of the MINI brand – British Leyland – pulled the plug on production of the Mini Cooper. It was then that Cooper snr. started making tuning kits through his company John Cooper Works, in order to meet the continuing demand for a "hot" MINI Classic.

It wasn't until 1990 that a Mini Cooper was put back on the market – on the initiative of Michael Cooper. By that time, his father had taken a step back from the automotive business, although he continued to stop by at the company every morning – almost until his death in 2000 – to chat with mechanics and customers. In 1999 father and son enjoyed a test drive in a prototype of the new MINI, and Michael's feedback subsequently helped the new development team to optimise the MINI. Since its launch in 2001, the new car has also been made available in the model and engine variants MINI Cooper, MINI Cooper S and MINI Cooper S with John Cooper Works Tuning Kit, with output of up to 210 horsepower.

John Cooper was extremely proud to see his son continuing the family tradition. As he scaled down his hands-on involvement in the business, he liked nothing more than chatting on the phone with fellow motor sport veterans like Jackie Stewart about the unfettered, daredevil early days of Formula One: about the car stunts, about getting one over on rivals, about the women and the parties – and, above all, about that night in Reims when one future world champion climbed into a tree and another was standing below.

Rauno Aaltonen

—

The rally professor

"Thinking is the key" is Rauno Aaltonen's advice to even the most untalented drivers for dealing with any situation on the road. And his demonstration model of choice for 40 years now has been the MINI.

— By Jürgen Lewandowski

Left: Rauno Aaltonen in his racing gear. A first-class analyst and shrewd operator, he is capable of interpreting the vibrations of a car to the finest detail.

Below: Four-wheeled speeder meets the fastest of big cats. Rauno Aaltonen at the wheel of a Mini Cooper S during a rally in southern Africa. The cheetah is quicker over a short distance – sprinting from 0 to 100 km/h in just a few seconds – but will run out of steam after 500 metres.

Child prodigies are free from the normal shackles. They have no need to sell themselves at all costs; they are welcomed with open arms by gushing adults, can pursue their own ideas without interference and are free to make mistakes without being instantly derided or slated for their failure.

Rauno Aaltonen was a case in point. He began riding motorbikes and driving cars around his parents' back yard in 1944 at the age of six. At 13 he was lining up for his first motorboat race, his father – Finland's fastest motorbike rider before the war – having cheekily agreed that no, you would never have guessed his son was as old as the minimum entry age of 16. Three years later, Rauno was crowned both Finnish speedway champion and Scandinavian motorboat champion. But that was just the start. Aaltonen rode a Ducati to a grand prix victory in the motorcycle world championship and, at 18, also transferred his talents to four wheels in Formula Junior racing and the European Rally Championship. However, this breadth of success presented him with a dilemma – where should he focus his attentions from now on? Did his future lie with boats, motorcycles, car racing on the track or rallying?

"When you start racing at such an early age, you have the advantage of being totally fearless. Your older rivals had to deal with everyday stresses, problems at work and the like. I, on the other hand, could concentrate on my racing and practise

two to three hours a day. And I learnt from my father to meet every challenge with an analytical mindset." Indeed, motor sport and life in general have always represented primarily an intellectual undertaking for the now 68-year-old Aaltonen. If two motorboats were fitted with identical engines, you couldn't outpace the other in a straight line, you had to be quicker around the corners: "So I built the best-suited boat with the highest cornering speeds – and duly won races."

For the young Aaltonen the way forward was clear as day. You had to think of everything, sound out every probability and take care of every detail, yet without losing sight of the overall picture. He used his wide range of motor sport experience to develop an incomparable sense for racing on every surface, from gravel to ice. Motorboat racing had given him a feel for balance, bikes the ability to adapt to any type of engine – to "feel the vibrations", as he would say – and car racing the appreciation of a higher form of driving dynamics, a closed book to the "driver in the street". After all, what mere mortal would have it in them to roar at the absolute limit over the sheet ice of the Col de Turini in the Maritime Alps late at night and on nothing more than thin tyres with a few spikes?

By the age of 18, the young Aaltonen was already a pretty shrewd racing driver. Indeed, just two weeks after finally taking his road driving test the youngster drove a Saab (in the right hands, an almost unbeatable machine at the time) to third place in a 2,000-km round of the Scandinavian Rally Championship: "By the time I got to the finish line, the boot lid was about the only thing still intact. Practically all the special stages were new to me, and when that happens you always have to drive rather faster than is advisable. Anyway, you can always use the snow banks to take the edge off your speed if need be." And people used to say that he hated braking.

With his reputation for delving intensively into the secrets of driving dynamics, Aaltonen became known as the "rally professor". And today there are still only a small number of people who can explain the correlation between the polar moment of inertia and its effect on the leverage of rack-and-pinion steering systems in such a relaxed and entertaining manner. When, in 1960, he saw a MINI Classic for the first time in Finland ("It was a green 850"), this depth of knowledge – underpinned by theoretical principles compiled and internalised over a significant time frame – confronted him with the sudden realisation that here was the perfect rally car. "Small, agile, all four wheels positioned right in the corners, an optimum wheelbase combined with the smallest possible basic area and, above all, this sensationally low polar moment of inertia, which determines how light a car is to steer. As soon as I laid eyes on the MINI, I knew it was a winner."

However, the large Austin-Healey 3000 was still the rally representative of MINI Classic manufacturer Austin,

and Aaltonen was tied to the Mercedes-Benz works team. It was a contract he earned at the wheel of his father's old Mercedes 220SEb in the Swedish Rally of 1961, where he took around a minute every ten kilometres out of the typically well-organised Mercedes works team. Anybody able to humble Stuttgart's finest in this manner was worthy of the works contract which was waiting for Aaltonen the day after he crossed the finish line.

A year later, the British Motor Corporation (BMC), which owned both the MINI Classic and Austin-Healey brands, took a radical step. The company appointed Stuart Turner as competition manager and allowed the man Rauno Aaltonen still regards as the best rally competition manager of all time to take the MINI Classic into race action. Turner had already slipped Aaltonen his phone number at the Polish Rally of 1961 with the invitation to call if he ever fancied working together.

It was a hallmark Aaltonen trait that alerted Turner to his talents. Rally regulations exposed certain ambiguities when it came to calculating times, and where and when which times should be clocked in. Just to be on the safe side, Aaltonen – with his knowledge of Finnish, Swedish, English, French and German – had read the regulations in German, English and French and settled on his own interpretation of the rules (which turned out to be correct).

The deal was done, Aaltonen had a seat in the car he had identified as the theoretical ideal all that time ago, and was part of the most efficiently organised team of the time.

"The secret behind the run of success and the MINI legend is actually very simple. We had the best car, the best mechanics, the best preparation and the best co-drivers: Englishmen. The story with the co-drivers was also typically Aaltonen. Too often he had misunderstood an instruction from whichever nationality of co-driver he had at the time. When you're driving at night or in fog, that can lead to some interesting challenges and unscheduled off-road excursions at the wheel. This led him to get in contact with the air force and study the phonetics which allowed them to avoid inaccurate interpretations. His investigations revealed that English – interspersed with vowels and with its word selection often reduced to just one or two syllables – significantly reduced the number of offs during a rally. So what better solution than to recruit British co-drivers?

Given this search for perfection, it was no wonder that Aaltonen grew into the star of the MINI scene and delivered a large number of the brand's key victories. As for his favourite win, that would be "the RAC Rally in 1965. As the rally leader, I was last to go on the final special stage. Ahead of me was Timo Mäkinen in an Austin Healey 3000. He had become stranded on a long incline which was, surprisingly, covered in snow. In an attempt to stop me from winning the event, he had then shunted his Healey across the road. To get around his car and seal the victory I had to use the embankment as a kind of high-banked curve. Unfortunately, I lost a serious amount of drive in the manoeuvre. I turned to my co-driver Tony Ambrose and said: 'Would you please get out and give me a shove?' This 'would you please' was crucial, as you don't get anywhere in

life by forgetting your manners. Tony got out of the car and promptly slid onto his backside on the slippery road surface. Back on his feet, he pushed the MINI Classic up the hill, while I did what I could to help with my foot pushing over the ground through the open door. Mäkinen was speechless; it was a great win."

Of course, the MINI Classic run of success had to come to an end, although Aaltonen swears blind that his "perfect rally car" would have continued to rake in the victories for a couple of years more given the right care and attention. Today, the Finn is a master drifter and his pupils still hang on his every word – and for good reason. After all, he has the ability to first explain the physics of any driving situation and then provide a practical demonstration of his point at the wheel. And he does it all with an inimitable and overwhelming charm and courtesy.

Below: The rally professor in his civvies at the wheel of his favourite car. He claimed his greatest victories with the MINI Classic. Today he uses his role as a MINI expert to introduce his audiences to the virtues of the current car.

The Oxbridge Race.

MISSION (IM)POSSIBLE –
HOW THE MINI
FOUND A NEW HOME

*A car factory has to move premises
in a matter of weeks. Cue for the removals trucks
to pound the roads day and night.*

BY: JOACHIM BESSING

*''Picking up the phone had set in motion
an inexorable chain of events. The countdown
started on the afternoon of March 16th, 2000, and
a year later the first MINI had to roll off the
production line a few floors below.''*

A single phone call transformed Paul Chantry's office into centre stage for an industrial thriller. Up to then, there had been nothing unusual about this unremarkable office on the upper level of a car factory. The phone on Chantry's desk wasn't red, just the same light grey as all the others on all the other desks in the building. And the soundtrack to the close-up of Paul's face was not Lalo Schifrin's unmistakable *Mission: Impossible* theme. At least not yet. However, the caller's message was very much of the "Your mission, should you choose to accept it" variety. A few minutes earlier, Chantry was the head of body production at Rover. Now he had been turned into the Ethan Hunt of MINI.

Standing up, he realised that for this particular case there was no time for his usual two or three glances out of the window, a coffee and a stroll over the yard. No time to admire the rolling countryside and old walnut trees backing onto the brick buildings of the factory, or the whitethorn hedges, just flowering nicely.

"We have the following task," he began shortly afterwards, his twelve best men gathered in front of him. "We are here," he said, pointing to a map of England on which a red pin marked the location of the Cowley plant on the outskirts of Oxford. "And the MINI is there." A green pin singled out an area near the deceptively close-looking city of Birmingham. "That's Longbridge. So far, so good. The Germans have a saying: 'Dem Ingenieur ist nichts zu schwer' – nothing's too difficult for an engineer. I fear this project, though, will be just that. Our job is to move the whole production facility for the MINI to Oxford. The decision has been made to build the new car here in Cowley."

None of his team was in any doubt that Paul was being serious. His face was as grey as his telephone.

"But that's not all. At the same time, the production machinery here has to be taken out and moved up to Longbridge."

"A swap," suggested Simon.

"That's about the strength of it," nodded Paul. For a moment, his mind appeared to be elsewhere. "Yes, a swap. There's no other way of doing it. We need halls for the MINI, but they're all in use as things stand." Paul continued his speech in hushed tones: "What makes the whole thing really difficult is that we're up against it timewise – not to mention in terms of costs. Let's start with the timing…"

Paul had arrived at the only element of his mission which had anything in common with the adventures of Ethan Hunt: a ticking clock. In Cowley, as on the silver screen, picking up the phone had set in motion an inexorable chain of events. The countdown started on the afternoon of March 16th, 2000, and a year later the first model year 2001 MINI had to roll off the production line a few floors below.

While Special Agent Hunt is frequently involved in a race against time in his battle against evil, the task of Paul Chantry's team was quite the opposite: to make something good happen, and in doing so avoid anything else grinding to a halt.

Until that phone call, the MINI had been developed in Longbridge. The pilot run for the new MINI models was already being produced in small unit figures at the Midlands plant in order to run the rule over the quality of the cars. Not that the Longbridge factory was exactly a small-scale laboratory cobbling together a few one-off prototypes. Far from it. The systems in place at Longbridge – the same that had to be dismantled and transported to Oxford – constituted fully-functioning series production installations. If you've never looked around the inside of a vehicle manufacturing plant, it's difficult to imagine the quantities and sheer scope of machinery, technology and space required to carry out the job at hand.

Car production shapes our idea of modern-day industrial manufacturing processes. To the uninitiated, it instinctively conjures up images of long assembly lines, with people and robots splitting the bodyshell work. The cars take shape in a linear process consisting of a logically organised, clear sequence of stations at which one part after another is added until a finished car emerges at the end.

The reality, and it was the harshness of this reality that turned Chantry's face a worrying shade of grey, is very different. If automotive production still worked along similar lines – literally – as in the past, if it followed this linear progression that we still envisage today (of a factory made up of clearly-defined assembly lines), cars would be unaffordable and an infrequent sight on the roads. But moving all the hardware would be rather more possible. In a similar way to the sections of a wooden train set, you could dismantle a long assembly line section by section, pack it neatly into trucks, drive it 70 miles down the motorway to Oxford, put it back together in the right order and have MINI production up and running in no time.

Although the production process for the MINI still follows the linear principle – an unbroken work flow from A to Z sees only a few hours pass from the moment a robotic hand grabs the first part to the application of the finishing touches – automotive pioneers of Henry Ford's generation would rub their eyes in astonishment at today's assembly systems. The aforementioned move from stage A to stage B takes place as part of a multidimensional process. If a journey down a river used to be a fitting comparison, today you're looking at a complex rollercoaster, albeit one which runs by the millisecond and with nanometric precision. The accuracy with which the robots apply their welding spots and execute their twists and turns is based on a tolerance of 0.05 millimetres, equivalent to half the diameter of a human hair.

Look through the eyes of Paul Chantry, a professional carmaker, and you would see 21st-century reality through sharply focused grey lenses rather than rose-tinted spectacles. Now, just as when Chantry's phone rang that day back in 2000, the inside of a modern-day production facility more closely resembles an overgrown garden. Only the last stage of production, the assembly shop, will remind you of those wooden train rails.

The bulk of the production process takes place at a stage known as the "body-in-white", a term which dates back to the early days of automotive technology. It describes the original appearance of the vehicle shell, when the pure metal – untreated back then, galvanised today – is welded together into the unpainted body. At this stage, the body does actually look white. In those pioneering years, the metal was dipped in a tank of white primer. Even today, the bare metal still shimmers brightly in the neon light.

In the early 20th century, however, there were no robots to carry out the spot welding and, above all, to haul around and lay out the numerous parts. But today's robots are not simply lined up in formation. While there is certainly no shortage of assembly lines in the body factory, they don't lead straight from one end of the hall to the other in a line long enough to cross a small village. Instead, distances are far shorter and the comparison with an overgrown garden is not as random as you might think. A collection of robots of this type – anchored in concrete foundations and fenced in like animals in a zoo – is known by robot manufacturers as a "robot garden".

Robots, by nature, tend to spark some romantic images. However, the models at work in a car factory have nothing in common with a chirping, whistling dustbin in the R2-D2 mould of *Star Wars* fame. They have no face, no legs, no camera eyes, no voice synthesiser, consisting instead of gigantic steel tentacles, each a couple of tons in weight. They weld and they grab, but conversationalists they are not. In fact they're not even silver, but painted in an irrepressible orange, rather like the road sweepers you see on the Continent.

Over 250 two-ton robots with the combined girth of two Sumo wrestlers in a clinch are quite enough to have your average removals company reaching for the white flag. To

These robots have nothing in common with a whistling dustbin in the R2-D2 mould. They are gigantic steel tentacles, each two tons in weight. They weld and grab, but chatty they aren't.

the untrained eye, there is no way all this equipment can be transported through what looks like a grade-A mess. The inextricably tangled jumble of assembly lines, transport rails, platforms, bridges and robot gardens running over, under and at eye level stretches back further than the eye can see.

Overriding all this, however, was the basic pressure of time. A full year might sound like a relatively long deadline for a move, depending on how much you have to pack and unpack. But Paul Chantry knew that the countdown had begun two months ago, time taken up working out a plan for how the transfer could possibly be achieved. Then you have to take away the three to four months required – in an ideal world – to optimise the production processes to the point where the MINI could roll off the production line at the new location on time. And that, of course, is all assuming that the equipment had arrived safely in Oxford and whirred smoothly back into life.

It was now July, and midway through a summer that had been unusually wet even for the UK. But the weather wasn't the only problem. The hall where the Rover production kit had just been disassembled, and which was to accommodate MINI production, turned out to be in serious need of a spring-clean. The scheduling had become so tight during the two months of planning and the pressure so unyielding that there was only one possible solution – one based on the same principle as the performance artist who could juggle three running chainsaws at the same time. Starting from the fourth floor of the huge hall, a first column of technicians worked their way down towards the ground floor and dismantled the old production systems. At the same time, a second team of specialists set about cleaning the walls, while a third group rolled in the MINI production machinery. And, as if there wasn't enough going on, a fourth band of workers were erecting a new roof for the hall over the existing one.

To an extent, all car production facilities are similar in nature. However, the equipment built in Longbridge for the MINI required a hall which was rather taller inside than the one available in Cowley. As the robots and other equally expensive machinery were already in place there, the classical solution of simply raising the level of the roof was not an option. Given the damp weather that summer, nobody wanted to risk leaving all that technology open to the elements for even half a day.

The stream of trucks hammering down the M40 was interrupted for no more than a few hours during the night. Loaded with robots, assembly lines, bridge sections and other machinery needed for MINI production in Oxford, the fleet numbered 300 HGVs. It was August by the time the final load had been unpacked and all the machines were at last installed in their new home. However, not a single robot had yet been programmed and none of the assembly lines had moved a muscle. Barely five months remained until the start date for MINI production.

It was a snapshot in time that would go down in automotive history as "The 129 days of Oxford".

On the morning of the first of those 129 days, Paul got into his car and drove through the vast expanses of the hall. Never again would it be so bright, so quiet and – apart from the robots gathered in the middle – so empty.

By midday, the first stage of work was well into its stride. Robot developers Kuka had scrambled 160 employees for the mission, including 30 programmers. The robots were mounted in concrete foundations, while all around them the workers from a construction contractor set about laying the new flooring for the hall. The floor was a light grey colour, surely an unusual shade for a factory floor. You'd think, after all, that a brown surface would be more practical and better suited to its purpose, able to cover up some of the dirt and oil. However, German engineer Rainer Bickmann, who was at Longbridge overseeing the preparations for the MINI launch, saw things quite differently: "How else would I be able to see if the floor was really being kept clean?" he asked Paul Chantry.

Bickmann, who would later also take over responsibility for final assembly, had a test assembly facility erected on a secluded area of the plant site. This – another hall with a light grey floor – would be the training venue for the individual assembly sequences using the relevant machines. Already in place was the jokingly christened "Glue Boy" robot, whose sole task is to apply a squirt of adhesive to a specially formed material which can then be pressed carefully to the inside of the MINI roof. This material minimises the vibration noises coming from the roof. It's important that this blind, one-armed robot carries out its task with absolute precision 250 times a day. Away from the noise of the build-

*Starting from the fourth floor of the
huge hall, a first column of technicians worked
their way down towards the ground floor
dismantling the old production systems.*

*If you're in a race against time,
perhaps the only policy is to work with the clock.
Or at least try.*

ing site, Bickmann's test assembly allowed these complex adjustments to be carefully rehearsed.

If you're in a race against time, perhaps the only policy is to work with the clock (or at least try) – i.e. cut down on breaks and minimise quiet patches when you're more likely to notice how little time you have. The team had been working seven days a week since that afternoon in March. The solid core around Paul, meanwhile, had been whittled down to six people. Those left were now responsible for the construction of the final assembly hall, the paint shop, coordination of logistics with suppliers and a host of other key areas involved in putting together the "miracle plant" called MINI.

"It was no time for joking and frivolity," recalled Paul Chantry. On one occasion they went into Oxford together, spending a brief evening in Bath Place, the 15th-century restaurant whose guest rooms once played host to a rendezvous between Liz Taylor and

The final obstacles were negotiated almost unnoticed, such as a new heating system fitted in double-quick time alongside production of the test series – minor details compared to the major challenges now behind them.

Richard Burton. That was a very different era. Burton was starring at the Playhouse theatre and a Mini Cooper stormed to victory in the Monte Carlo Rally. The team used the evening to try and unwind for a while. Simon pointed out the irony of the German Bundestag's own large-scale relocation to Berlin the previous year. He had brought a newspaper cutout in which it was reported that "11 kilometres of files" were moved from Bonn on the Rhine to Berlin on the Spree. It was enough to provoke a tired smile or two around the table.

"Tell me, Paul," enquired Simon "has anybody ever done anything on this level before?"

"What, relocated a body factory?" replied Paul. "No, not that I know of. Under normal circumstances you leave things where they are. You can always take final assembly somewhere else, though. That happens quite often. But then you send the bodies off, not the factory!" Paul changed the subject. "Did you ever use to watch that TV programme *You Bet!* where people showed off their unique skills in front of millions of viewers? Everything from blowing up hot-water bottles until they exploded to identifying aircraft by their smell. I'd go as far to suggest," he added in his inimitably polite way, "that we could qualify for a millennium edition of the programme." There was no sniggering, just nods of agreement all round. This was, indeed, no time for joking.

Final assembly test runs got underway in September. In Longbridge, a few hundred bodyshells had been stockpiled, which were now transformed into fully-fledged MINI cars. These were magical moments and gave the occasionally ruffled team an enormous boost. It wasn't easy for them to wait for the start of series production of a model none of them had ever actually laid eyes on. Seeing it "in the flesh" provided the motivation they needed to get through the long wait. The fact that BMW Group put its investment in Oxford at almost 200 million pounds further increased faith in the small car, and the launch of the initial ad campaigns raised anticipation to a whole new level once again.

The final obstacles were negotiated almost unnoticed. The light in the assembly hall, for example, turned out to be inadequate, meaning that work during the grey autumn months had to be wrapped up early every day. Plus, a new heating system had to be fitted in double-quick time alongside production of the test series. But these were all minor details for the team: the major challenges were now behind them. The true *You Bet!* moment came with assembly of the EMS rail-guided transportation system. Made up of interconnecting rails and measuring many hundred metres in length, this system is designed to transport body components along the underside of the hall roof. For safety reasons, the rail assembly could only be fitted once production had already already started on the hall floor. The engineers cautiously moved between the robot gardens on mobile lifting platforms – both above and below it was a matter of ensuring those famed 0.05 millimetres would be kept to in all areas.

Oddly enough, none of those involved in this extraordinary project remotely talked about a miracle when, after exactly 129 days, series production began and – on April 26th, 2001 – the first MINI in classic Chili Red rolled off the production line in final assembly. There's no doubting it was a miracle, but the men and women who made it possible were not used to thinking in terms of supernatural forces in their professional lives. They work within the limits of possibility, trusting in calculable factors and their own engineering skills. They proved that old German saying that "nothing's too difficult for an engineer". They made sure that the original plan following the phone call in March – a suicide mission if ever there was one – was brought to fruition bang on time. The entire inner workings of a car factory were relocated from Longbridge to Oxford within the space of a year, the machinery was put back into service in its new home, and the scheduled launch date was successfully met.

Paul "Ethan" Chantry savoured the experience of finally being able to close his office door behind him in the knowledge that, for the next half-hour at least, nobody else would be disturbing him. And, for the first time in a year, he looked out of the window again. The whitethorn was in particularly fulsome bloom after all the rain. Time to catch up on a spot of sleep. At the weekend, perhaps. Mission accomplished.

*They were magical moments
that gave the occasionally ruffled team
an enormous boost.*

From the
Original
to the
Original.

When the new MINI, the successor to the MINI Classic, came onto the market in 2001 the jury was very much out on whether it could tap into the spirit of the time and have a lasting effect on the motoring world. In the event the anxiety was shortlived, the new MINI proving to be a resounding success. Chief among the reasons behind the impact of the car – alongside its outstanding handling characteristics – was its irresistible design. The 1959 original served as the template for the new car, the designers packing all its spirited yet understated style, cheekiness, vivaciousness and energy into a 21st-century package oozing cutting-edge credibility. MINI fans prefer to set trends rather than follow the crowd and it didn't take long for them to show their approval. The new MINI represented the birth of a modern classic, bridging the gap from a much loved sixties icon to a new design original, one of the first of the new millennium. Now, five years on from its premiere, the engineers braced themselves for the next challenge: a subtle evolution of the 2001 MINI to meet a new set of requirements and add further weight to its maturity as a modern classic.

MINI design formula

$$d = \int \frac{(\text{Tech } \text{Erg } \text{Soz})}{t} \times D$$

form · individuell · arst. · 3/2/1 · funktion

Exterior
Facial expression

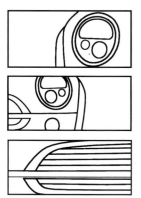

The unmistakably friendly yet striking face of the MINI is made up of a smile (the reinterpreted hexagon of the radiator grille), large round "eyes" (the headlights) and the fog lamps, playing the role of small beauty spots on its cheeks. The engaging character of the MINI shines through – and the world has been smiling back for almost 50 years now.

The evolutionary "from the original to the original" design philosophy has been adhered to faithfully from the 1959 MINI Classic through the MINI of 2001 right up to this latest MINI. The strategy includes numerous design icons from the MINI Classic, such as the round headlights, fog lamps and hexagonal radiator grille.

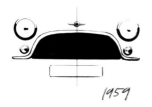

1959

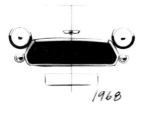

1968

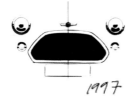

1997

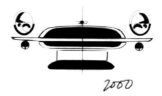

2000

2006

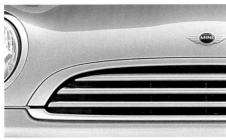

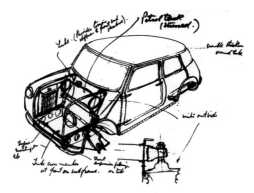

The hexagonal radiator grille is synonymous with MINI through the ages. After the split grille of the 2001 MINI (2. from top), the new model returns to the single-piece format of the MINI Classic (top), strengthening the status of this iconic design feature. The surfaces of the front end are now (below) tauter and its constituent elements given a cutting-edge yet evolutionary update. The car exudes a powerful and masculine allure in all its guises.

Form follows function: over the course of the decades Raymond Loewy's legendary dictum has become probably the most famous mantra in the history of design. Despite his theory's frequent brushes with doubt and scepticism, there are plenty of design icons the American could now point to for vindication. The MINI, for example, has represented a yardstick in terms of function, practicality and the use of space since it hit the roads almost half a century ago. And its form has, more than likely, only been able to survive for almost half a century because its unflashy functionality has steeled it elegantly against the tides of passing fashion.

This has allowed the MINI to turn its rejection of aesthetic superficiality into a success story of design, its undeniable functionality lifting it above all class barriers on its way to a classless preeminence. Enriched by against-the-odds sporting victories, the path to success became inevitable. After all, there's nothing more beautiful than the victory of the underdog over its supposed superiors.

The problem with standard-bearers, however, lies in the tendency of their admirers to idealise them. Every change is therefore viewed with suspicion, every step forward questioned. The original is the benchmark against which every further development is measured. This is where the wiles of the designers and engineers are called upon to bring the legend seamlessly up to date.
It was with great sensitivity and an even greater understanding of this pillar of British history that MINI was able to capture the essence of the car and lend it a fresh interpretation, but without losing contact with its heritage.

The MINI design team was clearly faced with a formidable challenge, a perilous balancing act between the past and the present. It was a question of extracting the original car's genes and fortifying them with the tools to handle the demands of 21st-century motoring. Everybody loved the unpretentious chassis of the 1960s classic, of course, but today we also demand rather more in the way of comfort. And while we hang on to memories of that tight and cosy interior and the lusty 4-cylinder engine – in its day such an irrepressible customer – today's safety and emissions standards require a rather different set of dimensions. No modern-day car can be complete without crash zones and a pedestrian-friendly bonnet, airbags and a powerplant prioritising economy and environmental compatibility. The MINI engineers' job was to combine all that with the legendary go-kart driving sensation that has always been a hallmark of the MINI experience.

Exterior
Dynamic orientation

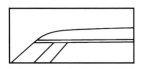

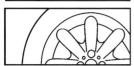

A car is an object and a space in equal measure, but it is also a piece of mobile architecture. The character it projects is described by the lines and proportions of its design. The taut design language of the MINI evokes the idea of unshakable solidity. Its silhouette adds visual emphasis to the car's formidable roadholding and at the same time maintains a classical harmony.

A character trait of the new MINI is the glazed section of the passenger compartment – the "glasshouse", as it is known. Like a dark wraparound band, it conceals the body pillars and fools the eye into believing that the roof is actually floating. The smoothly rising waistline is higher than on the 2001 model – by 18 millimetres at the rear – and serves to highlight the body's powerful stature. This distinctive element underlines the dynamic character of the new MINI.

From the side, the new MINI cuts a sharp, striking figure. Large wheels and minimal body overhangs at the front and rear give the car the impression of resting on its wheels. This "wheel-at-each-corner stance" has been a hallmark feature of the car through the decades, from the MINI Classic (top) to the latest model (below). Another tribute to the 1959 original is a diagonal body joint between the bonnet and side indicator, a fresh interpretation of the clearly visible welding seam in the same place on the MINI Classic.

Looking at these stipulations, you might be tempted to coin a new design mantra: "design follows rules". But that would be stretching the point a little. As a MINI designer maintains: "The designers' creativity still has the upper hand. When you get an image of the wonderful 1959 original and think about how completely it hit upon the zeitgeist of its era, then our task is clear: to find the right balance between the charm of the MINI Classic and the demands of today's much more discerning clientele."

The new MINI therefore retains the unmistakable silhouette, characteristic radiator grille and wheels located at each corner, a design feature which has always played its part in ensuring the car's fantastically peerless handling. The MINI has a stance arguably quite unlike that of any other car.

Although the new model has the same wheelbase as its predecessor, it is actually almost six centimetres longer – a concession to the guidelines governing safety provisions for cyclists and pedestrians. These extra centimetres of deformation capability will save lives and reduce the severity of injury.

As well as improving safety, part of the motivation behind these subtle revisions to the front end was to give the MINI a more grown-up, masculine look: "Our aim was to make the car even more muscular, to lend it a sportier edge," in the words of the MINI designers, and the new front end with larger bonnet is one of the key elements in understanding the new car: "It demonstrates the increase in strength and power in an understated way and offers an enticing preview of the new, more powerful engines under the lid." Setting the seal on the new front end and nestling like diamonds in the bonnet, meanwhile, are the new xenon headlights.

The enhanced dynamics of the new car are also due in part to the slightly raised shoulder line, which lends the once again fully glazed body that typically MINI feeling of lightness and flowing elegance. The new model also includes an enlarged rear window and thus improved visibility.

However, the art of design lies in preserving the roots of design icons as well as making those vital steps forward. Indeed, the typical horizontal division of the rear end, which helps the MINI to achieve its hallmark grip and stability, has been retained while the single-piece front grille – sticking closely to the form of the MINI Classic – makes its return. In the eyes of the MINI design team, this development is "not only a tribute to its past, but also the perfect link to the present. The time is right for these kinds of solutions."

Exterior
Cascading

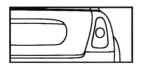

The parallel horizontal lines and flowing cascade of the MINI design bring power, stability and an engaging elegance to its rear section as well. From both a horizontal and vertical perspective, the rear lights – with chrome surrounds on the new MINI – are one of many gem-like details of the latest model.

As design icons, the rear lights remain virtually unchanged. Somewhat larger than on the outgoing model, they are now framed in chrome surrounds, giving them an even classier and more powerful presence. The gap between the rear lights and the slightly broadened "black band" on the lower edge of the rear has, however, been kept the same, lending the rear of the new MINI a compact silhouette despite its increased dimensions.

A MINI is still a MINI, as the passing of the generations shows. The MINI Classic (top), the 2001 MINI (middle) and now the new MINI (below) all see the individual sections of the car building on one another to give the MINI its solid stance. The design of the new MINI takes this cascade effect to the next level, making it clearly recognisable as a MINI from every angle and from its silhouette alone.

The new MINI is again adorned with lashings of chrome, another nod to its heritage. The MINI can pride itself on being the only car with a similarly long history not to have been sucked into the "plastic mania" of the 1970s and 80s which saw whole generations of cars stuck fast in the black mire. It was a fashion which MINI never bought into.

It's no wonder that the designers were easily influenced by this history. Indeed, they have not only increased the number of chrome elements for the new car but also given them extra presence, especially around the windscreen, rear window and radiator grille. The headlights and rear lights are also adorned with chrome surrounds, of course, giving them the appearance of precious stones set into the car body. The addition of chrome is a feature which carries particular resonance for MINI today in fulfilling the "from the original to the original" claim – perhaps for the very reason that it avoided being caught up in the whole plastic era.

It is understated considerations like the increased use of chrome, the finely-judged proportions governing the relationship of wheel-arch to wheel and the exact positioning of the front and rear lights which give the new MINI a balance between past and future probably unmatched in automotive history. The MINI designers are keen to cite the thin line between excessive devotion to the original and a misplaced taste for radical solutions promising only notional improvements: "We have to get the tonality spot on, to give the public the feeling that they're looking at a new car, but without detracting from design icons. All that makes it quite an art to retain the unshakable basic elements, yet also modernise and adapt them to the present day with understated alterations which may not be immediately apparent," says a MINI designer of the challenge involved.

No fewer than nine different prototypes were built internally and externally for the new design, providing clear evidence of how seriously the team had taken the task of creating a fresh interpretation of the MINI. In 2001 – at precisely the same time as the first successor to the MINI Classic was celebrating its world premiere – initial discussions began on the shape the car should take. And as the first new MINI since 1959 was quick to enjoy success, the debate shifted to other aspects of its design alongside the necessary technical and safety-related updates. For example, the search began for a globally credible and accepted form, one which would make a striking addition to the urban landscape of New York or Singapore, Beijing or Barcelona.

Interior & exterior
Circular elements

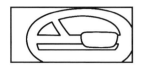

What do the MINI logo and MINI interior have in common? They integrate (masculine) parallel and (feminine) circular elements into the dashboard, door trim and centre console of the interior. The integrative design concept of the MINI has a new symbol: the Centre Speedo. The round central instrument not only shows the car's speed, but is also the display point for all entertainment and navigation functions.

The combination of circular elements – the instruments and air vents, for example – with the tautening horizontal geometry of the dashboard shapes the design language of the interior of the new MINI. This lends the whole area a refreshing spaciousness and light. The interior is sophisticated, solid and pure, exuding a premium character unique in this vehicle segment.

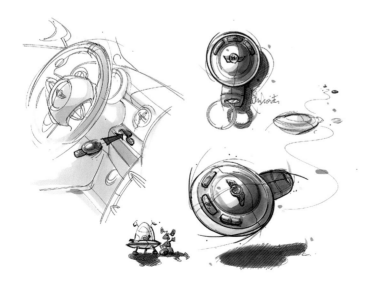

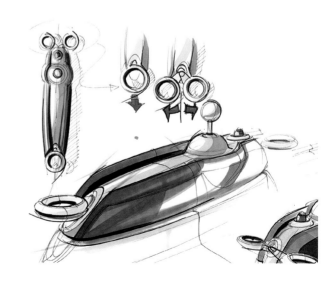

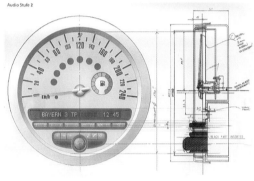

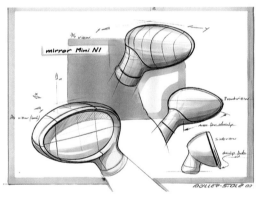
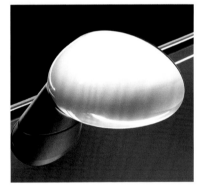
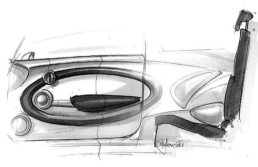

Circular elements on the exterior and in the interior are trademark design traits of the MINI. The headlights and wing mirrors are particularly distinctive features, while inside the car the Centre Speedo and door ellipses immediately attract the eye. Together with other circular elements, like the cup holder integrated into the centre console and the toggle switches, these rounded forms enhance the special cockpit atmosphere onboard the MINI.

"While taking into account the fondness for their original forebears, today's cars have to speak an internationally accepted design language, or better still boast a design language which influences the international perception of what constitutes good design," says a MINI designer, for whom the MINI is an example of global acceptance achieved: "The MINI has been given a warm welcome around the world, in almost every social stratum." That means a lot of fame and admiration, but also explains the extreme scrutinisation of its every detail. Does it fit in with the car's heritage? Does it bring the design another step forward? Does it secure the continuation of a success story?

Being taken to the hearts of people worldwide also has other implications. For instance, it leaves customers searching for a totally new form of individuality. Different tastes seek different forms with which to express their individuality. This desire for unique objects providing decorative allure and inspiring pride in ownership – shown most clearly by buyers for whom design is a key factor in purchasing a new car – places a huge amount of responsibility on the designers' shoulders. Indeed, design is a decisive element in the decision-making process of no less than 72 percent of all MINI customers, one of the highest values in the whole automotive business. It highlights once again the precariously thin line between two questions: "Why change a design which is already perfect?" and "Isn't it change that drives progress?"

There is an oft-quoted Latin saying "Tempora mutantur, nos et mutamur in illis" (Times change and we change with them), and it is probably this enduring realisation among the designers which continues to move the MINI on. They do this by giving the car a new edge and preparing it for the time when an earlier model can no longer exude the passion and strength which has allowed this brilliant design to survive through so many decades.

While the exterior of the MINI has grown slightly and become considerably more muscular for the reasons already mentioned, particular attention was also focused on the interior of the new MINI. The MINI designers like to refer to this approach as "evolution outside – revolution inside". It was a decision based, on the one hand, on the aforementioned trend towards individualisation. But there was also the desire to build in more and more new features, systems whose significance could not yet be predicted when development work was beginning on its predecessor in the early 1990s. Who back then could have foreseen the mushrooming popularity of navigation

Interior
Horizontal orientation

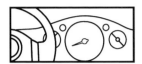

Squeezing maximum spaciousness out of a small area has represented the cornerstone of MINI interior design since day one. With the revolutionary, taut and horizontal geometry of the dashboard, the cockpit of the new MINI comes across as even larger and – in combination with the classic racing appeal of the circular instruments and larger chrome toggle switches, and the higher waistline – further enhances the much loved go-kart feeling at the wheel.

The revolutionary interior design provides the perfect complement for the evolutionary exterior. The raised window line of the exterior gives the interior a sporty cockpit feel, reinforcing the masculine character of the new MINI interior and the typical MINI go-kart feeling.

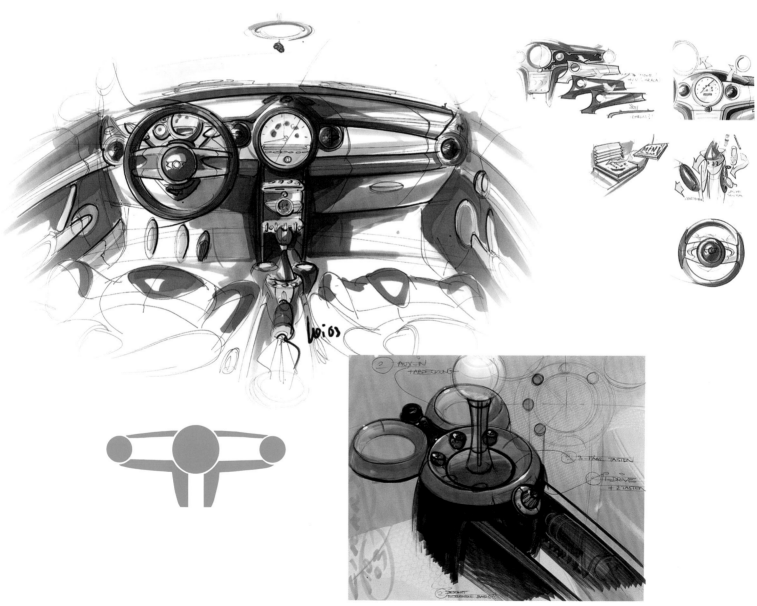

Sir Alec Issigonis could never have dreamed of technical features such as driver assistance or navigation systems in his brilliant original design (top), but today the interior of the MINI looks more like an aircraft cockpit (below). The horizontal emphasis of the cutting-edge dashboard creates a generous feeling of space in the new MINI.

systems, for example, or guessed that sophisticated stereo systems with CD changers or iPod connections would be a staple feature of the options list? One of the reasons for this development doubtless has its roots in the restricted space for cars on the roads of large cities. A MINI allows you to weave your way through the traffic as if you're in a go-kart. You can nip back and forth from lane to lane, spot a parking space and claim it for yourself in a matter of seconds. And, if you have to mix it with the masses every day in this urban maelstrom, you might as well do so in comfort and with a spot of luxury.

At the same time, the need for personalised living spaces has also gathered pace. As a result, the design and feel of the interior had to take on new qualities and at the same time open itself up to the desire for individual expression. "We now have a situation where almost every MINI on the road is a one-off. The likelihood of ever finding two identical models is virtually zero," according to one MINI designer. The interior is not only significantly more spacious and comfortable than before, it can also point to a wealth of top-class materials which create an ambience previously the preserve of vehicles a class or two above. To achieve this, the designers turned to fine textiles and exquisite leather, as well as wood, aluminium and premium paint finishes. This range of materials also allows a greater scope of interior variants to provide the perfect match for customers' requirements. And while in days gone by, any number of clever puns sprang up to describe the space inside the car (e.g. MINIature), the new MINI has clearly outgrown such affectionate quips.

The interior is frequently an area where the tricky balancing act between an illustrious past and a glittering future comes to the fore – and its design was naturally the focus of long and intensive discussions. "After all, it is the classic design icons, like the centrally positioned speedometer and the toggle switches on the centre console, which have shaped the face of the MINI from the outset." It was therefore clear to the MINI design team that making any changes here would be very much taboo, but that didn't stop them from giving these classic elements a fresh slant. Displays for the radio, CD player (which is stashed away neatly in the glove compartment) and navigation system add extra depth to the trademark analogue speedometer.

The toggle switches, meanwhile – now rather larger and more user-friendly – are spread over both the centre console and the roof lining, giving the driver the feeling of sitting in an aircraft cockpit. The increasing number of new functions meant the

Colour & trim
Maximum personalisation

The need for made-to-measure living spaces continues to gather pace. An extensive range of individualisation options when it comes to paintwork and materials ensures that identical twins are even more of a rarity in the MINI world than in real life. It's all about choosing your own style.

Sporty, classic, elegant or cheeky, MINI drivers can put their own personal stamp on their MINI with a choice of twelve different paint finishes. An extensive range of colours and materials means the imagination can be let off the leash inside the car as well.

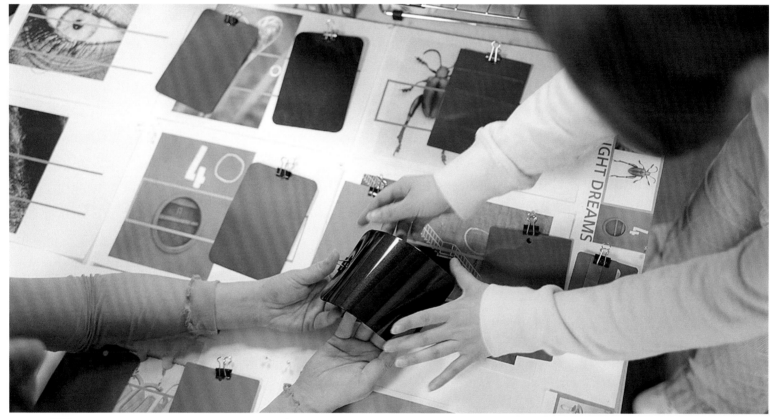

The individualisation process for the new MINI begins with the choice of interior specification and paintwork. A total of twelve body colours are available for the new MINI, eight of which are metallic finishes. New additions to the range are Mellow Yellow (see pictures of the formation process above) and Oxygen Blue. Chili Red and Pepper White have already adorned the outgoing model to stunning effect. Among the metallic options, British Racing Green, Pure Silver, Astro Black and the new Sparkling Silver, Lightning Blue and Nightfire Red shades all stand out. Plus, the metallic variants Dark Silver and Laser Blue can be ordered exclusively for the MINI Cooper S.

switches had to be divided up in this way, a solution not required in Sir Alec Issigonis' brilliant original design in the days when climate control and sound systems, driver assistance technology and navigation systems were not yet on the radar.

The MINI should always be recognisable as the heir to a great tradition, yet it should never become a slave to old memories. Perhaps that is the true secret behind its success. Remember – YES; extract the original's genes – YES; create a replica – NO. Those familiar with the MINI models over a long period of time will thus instantly recognise the typical horizontal shaping of the dashboard, a strong, powerful line extending even further through the air vents positioned at either end of the dash and creating extra space. And for those looking to experiment with the numerous interior fittings, this broad band – framed so elegantly by the dashboard cover and knee protection – can be accentuated with a splash of aluminium, or given a touch of British bar ambience with wood trim elements. These variations can, of course, be further enhanced by the careful selection of fabrics and leather, including piping and stitch colours, to fulfil every desire.

With all these considerations and the results they have generated, with the improvements and often painstaking process of fine-tuning, and with the progress which technology has delivered in recent years, the new MINI has without doubt entered a new dimension in terms of quality and equipment, enough to meet the most demanding requirements of a discriminating clientele. After all, today's customers expect features like satellite navigation, air conditioning, sound systems and the most advanced technology – features which a car with the heritage of the MINI simply has to offer. From day one, this was a car defined fundamentally by groundbreaking innovation. And the new MINI offers all these practical, safety-enhancing and life-improving solutions without ever neglecting the true heart of the MINI: the driving pleasure, the precise steering and go-kart cornering that puts a smile on your face, and the reassuring feeling of always having something in reserve.

Although the new MINI is every inch a state-of-the-art machine, it is not swayed by the vagaries of fashion, a philosophy the MINI designers are firmly committed to: "If you design a timeless object it is something you will never discard, because it will stand the test of time. That's the fundamental difference between design and fashion. Added to which, fashion is a cause of environmental problems, as sooner or later you have to throw it away." Which brings us back to the question of originality. Originals are prototypes, the initial drafts of extraordinary ideas. Ideas which, in the case of the MINI, revolve around the economical use of space and everyday practicality. Ideas

Colour & trim
Ambience

Simplicity and sophistication – it's a good match. The interior of the MINI emulates the understatement and quality standards of a tailor-made British suit and gives well-informed MINI fans a discreet hint of the car's identity. Indeed, it is possible you can tell just from the seat covers and the dashboard trim whether you're looking at a MINI One or a MINI Cooper S.

The interior is exquisite, solidly built and pure in appearance. It exudes a premium appeal unmatched in this vehicle segment. Customers can choose from Carbon Black, Gotham Grey, Tuscan Beige and Redwood Red for the interior, providing either a neat match or a stunning contrast with the car's body colour and trim elements.

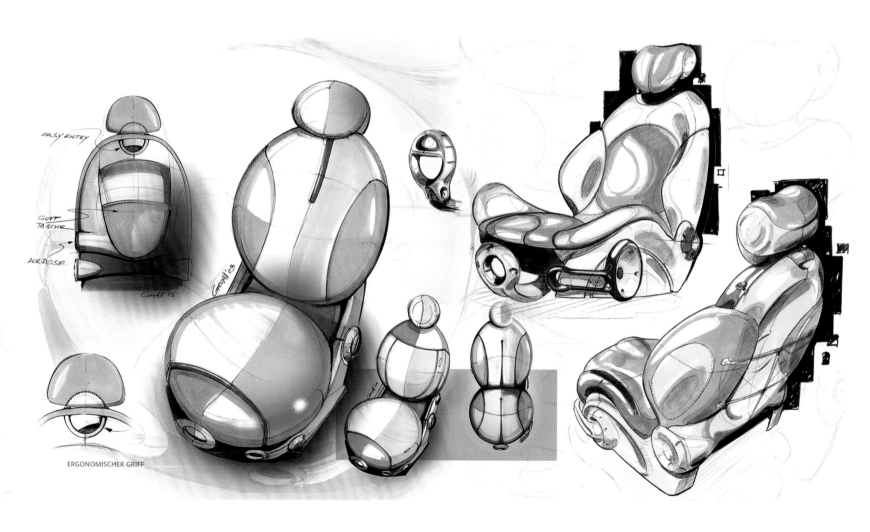

EASY ENTRY

SOFT TASCHE

LORDOSE

ERGONOMISCHER GRIFF

Accentuating the attention to detail of the new MINI, the optional Colour Line allows the cockpit to be shaped in the owner's own image. Colour accents in the lower elements of the dashboard spread through to the door panelling (left)and can be combined to pleasing effect with the materials available for the surface trim. Colour Line includes five shades – Dark Grey, Cream White, Pacific Blue (below left), Rooster Red (far left) and Mellow Yellow – and customers can take their pick from four exclusive surface trim variants: gleaming black piano lacquer, dark-brown oak wood, brushed aluminium or a gloss surface inspired by the structure of liquid metal.

which, as the design brief specified, are also tied in with the issue of aesthetics. And as the MINI – like any other physical object – is made up of lines in space, it was only logical that MINI should have ten of these typically MINI forms patented: formative design elements, such as the clear lines which define the car, determining its shape and its unmistakable character.

Good designers possess an intuitive understanding of the language of these lines and the form they create. "The relationship of these lines to each other is key," according to the MINI designers. At MINI, this means "the parallelism of the lines. Parallel lines lend stability to a form, keep it rooted to the ground. One of the reasons why we are so familiar with the MINI is that the new MINI has precisely the same proportions as the MINI Classic of 1959." Proportions which fit the template of the golden mean – the idea of harmony that goes back to the Ancient Greeks.

As well as following this parallel orientation, the MINI secret is also based on the considered use of circular and semicircular forms, forms which appeal to us not least because we are constantly confronted by them in nature in the shape of the sun, the moon, fruits and, quite literally, the eye of the beholder.

The second dimension therefore involved singling out circular forms and integrating them intelligently into the sound basis provided by the parallel lines of the MINI. The idea was to use positive convex curves, which gave the MINI a more muscular appearance than would have been possible with concave forms.

Customers opting for leather upholstery can choose from Leather Punch in Carbon Black (below) or Leather Gravity in Tuscan Beige. The touch of class provided by the classic Leather Lounge seat trim, meanwhile, comes courtesy of the brand's British heritage. Available as an option in two colour variants, it combines the traditional values of the brand with a cutting-edge design language. This exclusive piped leather (see bottom) is hand-stitched and its quality provides a feast for all the senses.

That just leaves the third dimension, for which the designers coined the term "island solution". Underpinning this area is the recognition that it is not only engineering considerations which determine how details of a car's design (e.g. the headlights, rear lights, wing mirrors, ventilation inlets and outlets, filler cap and ventilation nozzles) are integrated into its surfaces, but that aesthetics and the right proportions also play a key role. Whether the designers' term for this third and final insight has anything to do with man's age-old desire for his own private hideaway is debatable; but you could certainly consider the MINI a small but perfectly formed island, a place to escape to as well as a source of mobility.

—

By: Jürgen Lewandowski

MINI Concept
Frankfurt & Tokyo

"MINI is too good an idea for just one car" – that was the thinking behind the first MINI Concept, unveiled at the 2005 International Motor Show in Frankfurt. Innovative solutions to facilitate both getting in and out of the car and loading, highly functional details and the typically MINI twinkle in the eye make this concept car and its three siblings quite unique and point up the development potential of the MINI product range.

The MINI Concept Frankfurt (left) captures the imagination with its elegant, clear lines, side doors underpinned by parallelogram kinematics, split rear doors and a large glass roof, whose rear section slides away neatly out of sight.

The MINI Concept Tokyo (below) is equipped with a rash of playful details. Stashed away in the roof – and true to the car's "Go British!" ethos – is a picnic table complete with two chairs, while teabags and a Thermos flask can be found in the Window Box. The seat upholstery, meanwhile, is more akin to a British club armchair.

SIR ALEC
ISSIGONIS
100
BIRTHDAY
1906 – 2006

The Austin Seven Countryman (top) and the Morris Mini-Traveller "woodies" are the legendary precursors of the four MINI Concept variants Frankfurt, Tokyo, Detroit and Geneva (in descending order).

The MINI family looks forward to welcoming a new member – a unique vehicle concept with the individual attributes and smart solutions that will distinguish it as an independent character both within the MINI range and among the competition. That much is already signed and sealed. What the newcomer will be called and how exactly it will look, however, is still very much under wraps. The four major car shows – Frankfurt, Tokyo, Detroit and Geneva 2005-2006 – were allowed a glimpse of how things might turn out in the form of four variants of the MINI Concept study car. Needless to say, the MINI Concept harks back to the four-seater MINI Classic with expanded loading area and two rear doors which arrived on the market in September 1960. Badged initially as the Austin Seven Countryman and Morris Mini-Traveller, it was rechristened as the Mini Clubman Estate in its final guise of 1969. The MINI Concept is a snapshot of the future for both the MINI and automotive design in general. The car's target group are primarily customers looking for an unusual design and intelligent vehicle concept, while also valuing its everyday utility with their versatile leisure needs in mind. The typical MINI go-kart feeling and wide range of personalisation options will also appeal, of course.

The variant unveiled at the 2005 International Motor Show in Frankfurt served as the template for this study car. The basic concept was then combined with a fitting regional theme for its presentation at each of the three other venues. A principal aim was to make ingenious use of the room available. The MINI design team succeeded in retaining both the simple, tight form of the MINI body and its proportions. They also introduced a rather clever feature in the shape of the Concept's innovative door design, which sees the side and rear doors pivot out slightly to the side and then towards the front of the car in a single movement. Underpinning the concept is an intelligent door suspension system developed by the designers and engineers using parallelogram kinematics. In narrow parking spaces, for example, the doors open to create a wide entrance/exit or loading space while hugging the car body closely. The driver can then load large items into the rear with the minimum of fuss. An additional roof opening in the Frankfurt and Detroit studies allows them to accommodate even lanky pot plants.

But that's not the end of the MINI Concept story. Its powerful front end – including a classic hexagonal front grille and elliptical headlights – are further eye-catchers. And these are no ordinary headlights, as you discover when you switch on the engine and their "eyelids" open. The Cargo Box is another impressive feature, sitting flush in the boot floor and acting as a removable luggage compartment to accommodate all kinds of items which you'd rather not have open to prying eyes. Its lid doubles up as a sliding loading platform and can be used to manoeuvre heavy items easily into the car.

The interior of the MINI Concept has a light and airy feel. Anchored to the side of the centre console by special support arms, the driver's and front passenger seats appear to be floating in mid-air. The floor area under the seats is thus freed up to create extra room for the rear passengers' feet. One particular gem, meanwhile, is the mood function of the

MINI Concept
Detroit & Geneva

The MINI Concept Detroit (below) is the sports-minded variant and demonstrates the space in the car for sports enthusiasts to stow away their equipment. The ski rack on the roof, Window Box in the rear side window for various tools and accessories and the racy blue trim make the MINI Concept Detroit the sportiest of the four models.

The MINI Concept Geneva (bottom) is a tribute to the rally racing success of the MINI Classic. The Geneva variant is fitted out as a service barge, with design elements in red recalling the brand's victories in the Rallye Monte Carlo. The roof-mounted spare wheel, toolbox in the rear and the two auxiliary headlights on the roof showcase the flexibility and variability of the MINI Concept.

To mark the launch of the MINI Concept, HOFFMANN UND CAMPE VERLAG of Hamburg have published the book MINI CONCEPT FOR THE FUTURE.

rotating Centre Speedo. With the help of music, scents and light, this function allows the driver to create his or her preferred ambience. A whiff of fresh, stimulating grapefruit hangs in the air; fast, urgent beats bounce out of the speakers; orange light bathes the interior in a soft illumination. Together, these elements combine to create an ambience which makes the driver feel even more at ease inside the MINI. It is another step towards the individualisation of the car and the aim of giving each and every MINI owner their very own personalised automobile.

A start/stop element containing an analogue watch and the car key also plays an important role to this end. The driver inserts the key into the docking station in front of the gearshift lever, presses the starter button and the car springs into life. This key fob also allows drivers to programme in their individual seat positions, store mobile phone numbers and, of course, input their choice of music and moods. It's the perfect personalisation tool, especially if one MINI is driven by a variety of different people.

In addition to these innovations shared by all four of the MINI Concept variants, each model was also given its own specific character, particularly in terms of design. The Tokyo variant was developed under the banner "Go British!" in recognition of Japan's affinity with Great Britain. Like the Brits, the Japanese love a good picnic, so the MINI Concept for the Tokyo Motor Show came with a picnic table and chairs stowed away in its roof module. Cutlery and a salt shaker, meanwhile, could be found in the removable Window Box in the rear side window. "Functional solutions with a playful edge shape the face of MINI culture," say the MINI designers. In this spirit, the Tokyo study takes up a number of high-tech themes.

The MINI Concept was fitted with wintersports equipment for its presentation at the 2006 North American International Auto Show. Ski racks, goggles and gloves can be stashed away in the Window Box, while the sporty, bold blue trim includes wheel inserts, allowing drivers to put their own personal stamp on the car.

The MINI is an extremely sporty car, as demonstrated by the flawless handling and legendary go-kart feeling of every model. But the MINI Classic backed up its sporting prowess with a string of rally victories, never more impressively than in winning the Rallye Monte Carlo in 1964, 1965 and 1967. The fourth MINI Concept variant presented at the 2006 Geneva Motor Show is a nod to this celebrated rally racing past. The MINI Concept Geneva has a spare wheel on the roof and the Window Box fixed to the rear side window is designed as a toolbox. The front-opening bonnet complements the sporty profile of the MINI, the wheel arches and radiator grille combining with the bonnet to form a seamless component that swings forward and up, as on racing cars. The headlamps remain in the same position. This version of our MINI Concept creates a bridge between the modern era and the MINI heritage.

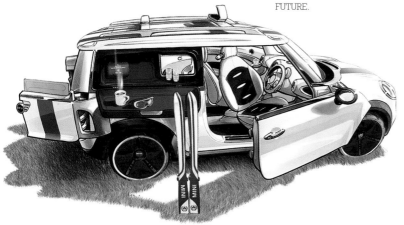

—

By: Peter Würth

Inspired by MINI.

More than just a car, the MINI regularly inspires fans, designers, advertisers and artists to come up with new ideas – unique and creative, humorous and exciting, innovative and breathtaking. You name it, the MINI has probably done it. It has hung precariously in mid-air, been redesigned from head to toe, chased down bad guys and broken records. One thing stands out loud and clear: being inspired by and having fun with MINI are two sides of the same coin.

MINI enters the Guinness Book of Records
400 MINI drivers converged on Italy's Lake Garda in 2004, making it the country's biggest ever gathering of MINI fans. In the courtyard of Villafranca Castle near Verona, 196 of them got together to form a 110-metre-wide MINI logo, setting a new world record in the process.

(4)

(1) Supersize MINI
The MINI XXL, featuring a flatscreen TV, DVD/CD player, minibar, leather upholstery, air conditioning, an intercom for calling the driver and a jacuzzi in the back, made its debut at the 2004 Summer Olympics in Athens.

(2) It's the taking part that counts
Inspired by the amazing feats of Olympic athletes, MINI buffs set their own official record at the 2004 Summer Games in Athens: 21 grown adults squeezed into a MINI Cooper, breaking the previous record of 20 and demonstrating once again just how roomy the MINI really is.

(3) MINI is into leather
The MINI is nothing if not cheeky, unconventional and tolerant, as this extravagant leather-clad MINI proved at the 2001 London Mardi Gras.

(4/5) Thumbs up for MINI fan hotels
Anything's possible with the MINI, even on occasion the apparently impossible. For example, for the Football World Cup 2006 in Germany, four MINI cars were converted into mobile "fan hotels" and sent to offer badly needed extra visitor capacity in the over-booked host cities. To ensure that every football fan really did feel at home during the competition, these MINI models were decked out in the national colours of Brazil, Italy and France, plus an international version for followers of other countries. Offering comfortable accommodation, the MINI provided World Cup and MINI fans from all over the planet with a relaxing – and stylish – night's sleep.

(5)

(1) Thrills and spills
Steeply-banked curves, 180-degree turns and wet landings in water troughs used to be thrills reserved for the leads in the action film *The Italian Job*. But since the summer of 2005, MINI fans can enjoy car chases galore in a rollercoaster MINI on The Italian Job Stunt Track ride at King's Island (Cincinnati, USA) and Wonderland (Toronto, Canada) amusement parks.

(2) Buckle up!
As if launched from a catapult, the MINI barrels from 0 to 100 km/h in just 9.1 seconds – pure adrenalin. No wonder MINI urged drivers in France to "Buckle up!" in 2003.

(3) Raging bull
In 2004, 25 cents was all it took for USA MINI fans to test-drive a MINI. A true alternative to good old-fashioned bull riding.

(4) Vroom with a view
In 2002, MINI toured the major cities of the USA – land of "big is beautiful", XXL, kingsize and big packs – perched on the roof of this massive SUV.

(5) Warning: radar speed trap!
In typical tongue-in-cheek fashion, MINI tipped off (speeding) Canadians in 2004.

(6) MINI takes the train
Ten Intercity and Eurocity trains whistled back and forth across Germany in 2002 with a life-size MINI Cooper S decal for good measure.

(7) Season's greetings from MINI
This unusual Christmas tree on the Thames was the MINI way of wishing Londoners a happy Christmas in December 2001.

(1) MINI takes to the air

The versatile MINI is capable of almost anything, even at the airiest of heights. At La Molina, a popular ski resort 150 kilometres north of Barcelona, Spaniards were astounded to see a MINI doubling as a gondola lift in the winter of 2005/2006.

(2) MINI with strings attached

This unconventional façade ad in Milan astounded Italy's MINI fans in 2005. A 160 kg, 1:1 model was rigged up as a moving yo-yo to demonstrate the remarkable capabilities of the MINI.

(3) Wake up the bull!

A gigantic advertisement with this imperative in March 2006 attracted lots of attention in Germany. By sending a text message, passers-by could transform the MINI Cooper S on the wall into a stomping, snorting bull.

(4) Gone with the wind

Look out for the gale-force airstream of the zippy MINI – that was the message of this 2003 billboard in the USA.

(5) Cutting corners

The most aesthetic connection between two points is a curve – or a MINI, as this fibre-glass Canadian MINI demonstrated in 2005.

(6) The sky's the limit

Who says you can only have fun with a MINI on the ground? In 2005, an Austrian Airlines Airbus A 330 emblazoned with the words "Attention! Pilot is a MINI driver!" showed that the brand's trademark sense of fun is equally at home above the clouds. The first to enjoy an exciting dash through the stratosphere were celebrities like Anastacia and Naomi Campbell, who were flown from New York to Vienna for the Life Ball.

MINI wears Bisazza

The creations of the Italian mosaic manufacturer Bisazza are considered the ultimate in interior design. Their elegant stones have adorned nearly everything imaginable: bathtubs, swimming pools and saunas, but also the dome of a mosque, a bank, and more than one bar in Milan have been graced with Bisazza tesserae. Since 2005, MINI has also been clad in Bisazza. Expert Italian craftsmen glued mosaics onto 5 MINI models, decorating each car with 37,000 glittering pieces. The results are nothing short of arresting, whether in pied de poule look (1), black-and-white checkerboard pattern (2), racy zebra stripes (3), a playful floral motif (4) or classic plaid (5).

Let me outta here!
This fibreglass MINI burst through the façade
of Johannesburg's Melrose Arch Centre in
2005 and ran for its life, just so it could finally
ride on the street.

(1)

(2)

(3)

(4)

(5)

MINI scores at the Life Ball

The Life Ball is the biggest charity event in Europe dedicated to the fight against AIDS. This lavish party brings together movers and shakers from the worlds of art, fashion, entertainment, business and the media. The Life Ball has been held in Vienna every year since 1993, and MINI has played an active part since 2001. In 2003, for example, a MINI designed by Angela Missoni (5) was auctioned on eBay for 33,050 euros, a MINI Cabrio / Convertible created by Gianfranco Ferré (3, 4) sold for 30,500 euros and, in 2005, a MINI designed by Donatella Versace and inlaid with Swarovski crystals (1, 2) went under the hammer for 120,150 euros.

Facing page: In 2006, the 38,150 euros netted by DIESEL CEO Renzo Rosso's Denim MINI Cabrio / Convertible (6–8, shown in picture 6 with supermodel Naomi Campbell) helped boost the total proceeds of the 14th Life Ball to over 1.1 million euros.

⑤

(1) Good as gold
In 1999, British actor Michael Caine asked his daughter, designer Natasha Caine, to come up with a new look for the MINI Classic. Her response: a black MINI Classic adorned with gold bars, as a homage to the cult film *The Italian Job*.

(2) Plenty of miles on the clock
For a 1999 design competition commemorating the 40th anniversary of the MINI, over 1,000 British MINI aficionados displayed their creativity by submitting a host of wacky design concepts. The winner: Mark Ward with his "Time Machine" MINI Classic.

(3) Diminutive model prefers MINI
"Mini" not only describes Kate Moss' wardrobe, but also her car: the British supermodel tools around London in a MINI Classic and even designed her own spiderweb-styled MINI Classic in 1999.

(4) Celebrity choice
From Twiggy and Enzo Ferrari to Peter Sellers, from the Beatles to David Bowie, almost every sixties celebrity worth his or her salt owned one or more MINI Classics. To mark the cult car's 40th birthday, artists and celebrities created their own personalised designs for the MINI Classic. David Bowie went for the reflective silver look.

(5) Madonna's camouflage MINI
Madonna loves MINI. The pop queen drives her own MINI Cooper and had a MINI outfitted in camouflage for her video *American Life*. Two days after the clip's initial airing, however, it was pulled for political reasons.

(1) Bean counts on MINI

Mr Bean is as English as warm beer, Big Ben, the Queen and the MINI Classic. In the eighties cult comedy series, comedian Rowan Atkinson as Mr Bean blithely piloted his Mini Cooper from one embarrassing mishap to the next.

(2/3) Agent MINI goes after the bad guys

Even Austin Powers, the spy with the screamingly loud wardrobe, drives a MINI. For his hit film *Goldmember* (below left) Canadian comic Mike Myers, who dreamed up the role of cult hero Powers, transformed six red MINI Coopers into racy secret agent vehicles embellished with the Union Jack.

(4/7) MINI steals the show

The most famous film featuring a Mini Cooper is doubtless *The Italian Job*, released in 1969 and starring Michael Caine as the small-time crook Charlie Croker (top left). The hit movie became a classic sixties cult film, with the 2003 remake also scoring a resounding success. In the latest version, American Mark Wahlberg plays the charming robber who escapes the police in a MINI Cooper packing a lot more horsepower (5/7). A total of 32 MINI models were recruited to film the nailbiting car chases.

MINI up in lights
For the 2002 Paris Motor Show, the French National Library was transformed into a gigantic 3,370-square-metre computer screen for displaying animated light installations. Among the themes featured was the MINI.

MINI
Community.

MINI CHALLENGE
—
Lifestyle meets Clubsport

The MINI CHALLENGE is a mixture of lifestyle event and Clubsport competition. Amateurs, professionals and celebrities line up on the grid around the world for this unique race series.

— By Christian Geib

It was a crisp January night in the winter of 1964, a night for heroes, a night for writing motor sport history. The setting was Monte Carlo, and the world's most famous rally was gearing up for the infamous "Night of the Long Knives" – the dash up to the 1,607-metre Col de Turini, the decisive and most demanding test of the Rallye Monte Carlo. Six Mini Cooper rally cars lined up for the stage to do battle with 290 rivals, some of which had more than twice their engine power. It was a perfect David versus Goliath scenario with Ireland's Paddy Hopkirk in a Mini Cooper S

up against the Swede Bo Ljungfeldt at the wheel of a Ford. However, in this meeting of unequals it was the Mini Cooper S that made best use of its strengths. Its small engine, agility and front-wheel drive allowed Hopkirk and co-driver Henry Liddon to rise as if on rails to the top of the overall classification. The final stage around Monaco's grand prix street circuit saw Hopkirk squeezing every last drop of performance from his Mini Cooper S. By the finish, the gravity of what had happened was thrown into stark relief: a little red David with a white roof had shown a clean

set of taillights to all the horsepower-packed Goliaths and swept to overall victory in the Rallye Monte Carlo. It was the beginning of a motor sport legend.

Over 40 years after the Mini Cooper S triumphed in the 1964 Monte, sporting prowess remains one of the key characteristics of the MINI. Its compact dimensions, wide track and long wheelbase see it roaring through corners in quite inimitable fashion. With such handling attributes, a career in race competition was a foregone conclusion, and it's no surprise that the

The go-kart feeling and flawless cornering, combined with reliability and superb handling, make the MINI the perfect racing car.

reincarnation of the MINI Cooper has featured in an increasing number of single-make series around the world since its arrival in 2001. One such competition is the John Cooper MINI CHALLENGE in Great Britain, which has captured the imagination of MINI fans. All the MINI Cooper S cars taking part in this series are fitted with the Tuning Kit developed by John Cooper Works.

From Belgium to Bahrain, Germany to New Zealand, the MINI CHAL-LENGE has long since become a fixture in the global racing calendar. The highlight of the series so far has been the impressive MINI festival held in Misano in the autumn of 2005, which attracted some 6,000 MINI fans from 40 nations to Italy. The World Final saw the 20 fastest drivers from the various national MINI CHALLENGE series lock horns to decide the official world champion, Belgian driver Maxime Martin clinching the title from Sweden's Fredrik Lestrup and the Austrian Johannes Stuck. "The MINI CHALLENGE is far more than just a single-make competition. It represents a whole lifestyle and brings a laid-back attitude and professional motorsport together under one roof," says one enthusiast who should know better than most: former touring car professional Alexander Burgstaller is today a brand ambassador for MINI CHALLENGE Germany and was his home country's inaugural MINI CHALLENGE champion.

One hallmark feature of the Clubsport series is the colourful mix of drivers. Talented juniors can pit their skills against experienced exponents of their craft and novice racers go bumper-to-bumper with former Formula One drivers. Indeed, the MINI CHALLENGE has also got the juices flowing among established racing drivers, with one-time F1 stars like Christian Danner, Jacques Laffite, Johnny Herbert and Marc Surer all embracing the challenge. Motor

Colourful contest: the MINI CHALLENGE brings together professional drivers such as Johannes Stuck (above), amateurs, celebrities and talented juniors.

Fair play first: sporting prowess and sportsmanship are the name of the game in the MINI CHALLENGE.

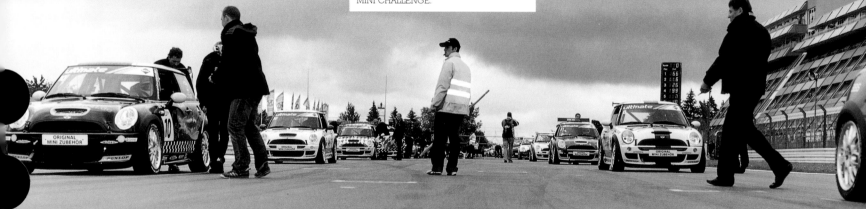

sport enthusiasts from the world of film and TV have also fallen under the spell of the MINI CHALLENGE and are frequent visitors to the grid as guest drivers. Anybody looking to enter the MINI CHALLENGE must be in possession of either the national A licence or international C licence.

Most of the cars involved in the German MINI CHALLENGE are entered by MINI dealer teams, who see the series not only as a sport-ing challenge but also as a platform for marketing and PR activities. As Burgstaller explains: "We share the same enthusiasm for an extraordinary car and a common passion for motor sport – that's more important than battling tooth and nail for every tenth of a second." And the MINI CHALLENGE stands apart from other race series in many other respects as well. A good example is the Paddock Lounge, "base camp" for drivers, teams, sponsors and guests. Step through the entrance to the tent and you will be greeted by easy-going chill-out music, while an expansive bar area, large plasma-screen TVs and cater-ing tailored to suit the event venue provide an international, typically MINI flair and relaxed atmosphere.

Sitting at one of the front tables is "Striezel" Stuck. The racing legend is giving his son Johannes a few final tips for the race: "You can stay on the gas a touch longer through the Castrol S." Two tables further into the tent and ex-Formula One star Keke Rosberg has met up with friend and former team-mate Jacques Laffite for a chinwag – a brief time out from the hurly-burly of modern-day F1. Indeed, four German MINI CHALLENGE races have taken place on the Formula One undercard in 2006: at the Imola (San Marino Grand Prix), Nürburgring (European Grand Prix), Magny-Cours (French Grand Prix) and Hockenheim (German Grand Prix).

The cars entered in the MINI CHALLENGE are based on the MINI Cooper S production model. Fitted with the John Cooper Works Tuning Kit, the race-trim MINI has 210 hp stashed away under the bonnet.

Safety first: the MINI CHALLENGE cars are fitted with racing kit including a welded-in safety cell, RECARO bucket seat, a five-point full-harness seatbelt, safety netting over the driver's window and a special braking system.

Equal opportunities: the MINI CHALLENGE cars are technically identical.

During the course of a race weekend, the MINI CHALLENGE area is not only a popular meeting place, it's also the venue for a series of events, from a design competition, model contest and sixties party to a stunt show starring Russ Swift (The Italian Job). The unique character of the MINI CHALLENGE is also anchored in the series regulations, with the emphasis placed on ensuring a level playing field. The drivers line up at the start with technically identical cars. Major components

such as the engine and transmission are "sealed" to prevent illegal modifications. And, in order to enhance the balance of the field even further as the season progresses, successful drivers are given a weight handicap for subsequent races. All these measures are designed to increase the appeal of the series for the fans. "There's no such thing as a dull race in the MINI CHALLENGE. Close battles and overtaking are the order of the day, and that's something I'm just

not used to anymore," admitted British former Formula One driver Johnny Herbert after a guest outing in a MINI Cooper S.

The close proximity of the spectators to the action is another key element of the MINI CHALLENGE concept. For example, the teams each have their own fully-fledged pit area in the Drivers' Club to which the fans have unrestricted access. Here, they can watch the mechanics at work on the cars and

immerse themselves in the high-octane atmosphere of undiluted motor sport.

With colourful sponsor livery, suspension lowered to leave the body hovering just above the asphalt, wide tyres and roof spoilers, the MINI CHALLENGE cars wear their sporting talent confidently on their sleeves.
The cars are based on the MINI Cooper S with John Cooper Works Tuning Kit, their supercharged 4-

cylinder engines developing 210 hp (154 kW). The powerplant teams up with the standard 6-speed manual transmission to allow top speeds of around 230 km/h.

The difference between the road and race-prepared versions of the car lies in the details. The MINI CHALLENGE racers boast a welded-in safety cell, a RECARO bucket seat with head protection, a five-point full-harness seatbelt, a fire extinguisher and safety netting over the driver's window to equip them as well as possible for the inherent risks involved in motor racing. An important safety feature, unique in this type of Clubsport car, sees the Anti-lock Braking System (ABS) retained in fully-functioning form and adapted to track conditions. And, in another exemplary move, the HANS (Head And Neck Support) system, which provides effective protection for the driver's head and neck area, has been made compulsory. The racing chassis of the MINI Cooper S has been tuned to the increased speeds on the track and can be adjusted perfectly to suit the demands of each individual circuit. The technicians have made sure that the basic chassis setting gives the car well-mannered handling characteristics.

By erring on the side of safety, they have ensured that the cars are also suitable for less experienced guest entrants, novice drivers and amateurs.

At first glance, the modern-day MINI Cooper S may have little in common with the 1964 rally car, but on closer inspection there's no doubt that its sporting pedigree is still alive and well. —

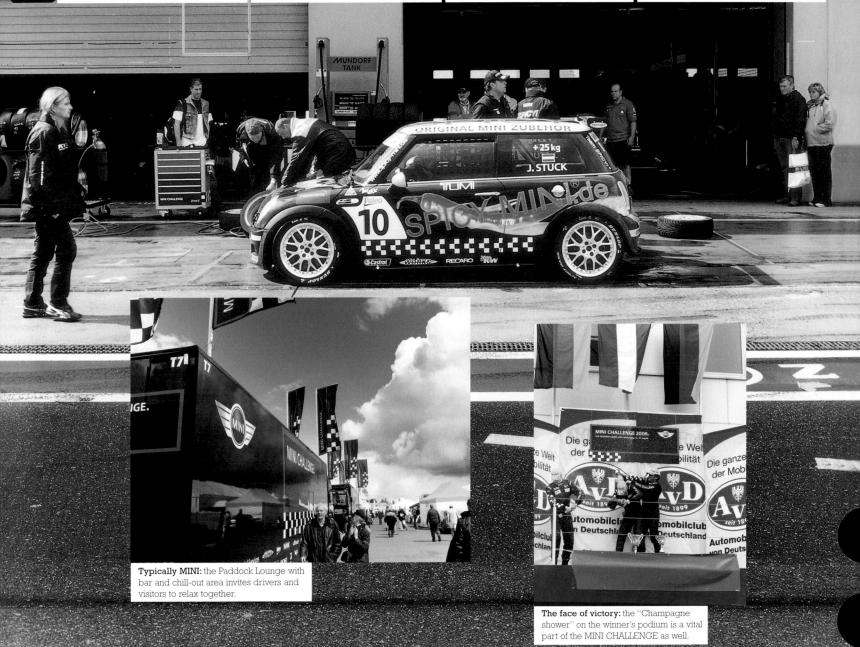

Typically MINI: the Paddock Lounge with bar and chill-out area invites drivers and visitors to relax together.

The face of victory: the "Champagne shower" on the winner's podium is a vital part of the MINI CHALLENGE as well.

MINI United
—
Friends. Festival. Challenge.

MINI drivers are not your average motorists. They are genuine enthusiasts and members of a worldwide community, and they meet up regularly at events such as Strahlung Pur in Germany, the international MINI Meeting organised by MINI Classic fans at different venues, MINI Mania in England, MINI Mucchio in Italy and MINI Takes the States in the USA. And, in 2005, some 6,000 MINI fans from 40 countries gathered in Italy for MINI United, the largest international MINI get-together yet.

— By Christina Reiffert

Alexander and his car wash team smile as they admire their handiwork. Freshly scrubbed and polished, the MINI Cooper S is just one shining example of the some 1,900 MINI cars from 40 countries which have come together at the MINI United event in Misano, Italy – the world's largest international MINI meeting. "It's been a while since it was last that clean," smiles the now even prouder owner Andreas. The car wash trio have done a great job, but the service isn't entirely free of charge. "The MINI fans also have to do something for us," explains Alexander. Andreas from Germany, for example, serenaded the team in recognition of their efforts, while Maltese enthusiast Steve – the driver of a red MINI Cooper S Cabrio with the aptly customised licence plate "S" – performed an impromptu dance and a Dutch visitor persuaded the crew to get their sponges out with a display of acrobatics. "MINI fans are great," beams Alexander. "They're creative and have some

wonderful ideas." It's certainly worth making that extra effort for the MINI United event, as fans can take their own MINI out onto the race track or put themselves to the test in a safety training course. And it's all the more fun in a freshly valeted MINI, of course.

But it's not just the shiny and gleaming examples that turned heads. MINI cars in every colour, and with a number of distinctive paint jobs and designs, were on show. Among the highlights were the special-edition Bisazza MINI, which was coated with over 30,000 shimmering glass stones by the Italian mosaic design house, and the MINI in floral Missoni look created for the 2003 Life Ball in Vienna. They were joined by the red XXL stretch limo and cars designed by Paul Smith and David Bowie. The MINI models displayed by the designers and artists were certainly attracting a lot of attention, but countless creations by ordinary MINI fans – cheeky, sporty or extravagant, depending on where

you looked – also captured the hearts of visitors from every corner of the earth.

Russian MINI aficionados Dimitri and Andrey drove their blue MINI Cooper S all the way from Moscow via St Petersburg, Helsinki, Stockholm, Copenhagen and Munich to the Adriatic, covering 3,600 kilometres in the process – the longest journey of any participant in the event. "We're a bit tired out from the journey, but we'll be savouring every moment and probably not going to bed too early," promised Andrey.

Another attraction at the event were James Piggin and the other 79 participants in the Italian Job Tour. "The Italian Job Tour is a charity rally across Europe. In years gone by, only MINI Classics were eligible, but we've also opened the doors to the new MINI over the last few years – it's all for a good cause, after all," says James with a twinkle in his eye. The Tour has collected over £1.7 million since 1990. "With the help of the 2005 Tour and MINI

United, we're hoping to break through the two-million pound mark soon," said James optimistically.

Alongside the MINI enthusiasts from the British Isles were 50 cars from the Greek MINI clubs, for whom Misano was little more than a hop across the water and a quick car drive away. MINI United was just one of a string of events the group were taking in during their trip. Next up for the Greeks – after a few laps on the karting track, racing "taxi rides" on the Circuito Santamonica and a delicious plate of pasta in the large party tent – was the world premiere of the new MINI Cooper S with John Cooper Works GP Kit. Limited to a production run of 2,000, this MINI develops 218 hp. However, it isn't the greater horsepower that makes the difference in this finely-tuned athlete: the two-seater's enhanced performance is due primarily to its lower weight.

The MINI Classic owned by David from Germany had 100 hp less under the bonnet, but the

(1) The kart track at the Circuito Santamonica. (2) MINI fans on their way to Misano. (3) Undiluted go-kart feeling. (4) Ex-Formula One driver Alessandro Zanardi wins the VIP race. (5) Exciting overtaking in the MINI CHALLENGE World Final. (6) Mike Cooper presents the MINI Cooper S with John Cooper Works GP Kit. (7/8) Safety and fair play take top priority at the MINI CHALLENGE. (9/10) The drivers lined up in identical MINI Cooper S cars. (11) The captivating stunt show thrilled the fans.

(12) MINI aficionados brought along their home-made creations, from cheeky to extravagant. (13) Party time at MINI United. (14) The presentation of the MINI Collection. (15) Greek MINI fans in Misano. (16) Mike Cooper with his band Dead Grateful. (17) The car wash team gave the fans' cars extra shine. (18) 1,900 MINI cars from 40 countries met up in Misano. (19) David Bowie's silver MINI Classic and the striped model designed by Paul Smith.

designer was still very proud of his car. "My boss gave it to me as a bonus after completing a successful project at work. However, it was built in 1978 and, by the time I got hold of it, had slipped into pretty dodgy condition. Together with a few friends I had to completely take it apart, buy a few spare parts and put it back together again," he explains. "The car's now worth 12,000 euros and its 120 hp engine has got me from Germany to Italy in one piece."

Although David proudly shows off his MINI Classic, he can't resist sneaking the odd glance towards the tuned Hot Orange MINI Cooper S Cabrio / Convertible with exclusive interior design owned by 25-year-old Sarah from Rimini. "A MINI Cooper S Cabrio / Convertible with John Cooper Works Tuning Kit would be the ultimate dream for me," admits David. Ho Hang On, howev-

er, has now seen his dream come true. The MINI fan from Hong Kong is the lucky owner of the 700,000th MINI, an Electric Blue Cooper S, which was symbolically presented to him at MINI United.

With classic models, creations with "gullwing" doors and 240 hp, Halloween specials, cars with trailers and others sporting wood panelling, there was something to suit every taste at MINI United. Indeed, it wasn't only horsepower, tuning and design aficionados who flocked to the event; fashionistas and music lovers were also well catered for. A MINI Lifestyle Collection fashion show presenting the latest trends was complemented by an exhibition displaying the best entries from the MINIInternational Photo Awards, while Mike Cooper's band Dead Grateful, singer Luca Dirisio and well-known British DJ Sonique

brought the tent to the boil after sundown.

The sporting highlight of the event came on Sunday morning with the MINI CHALLENGE World Final, which saw the 20 fastest drivers from the ten international MINI Clubsport series pit their skills in an unusual contest of four different disciplines – track races and a slalom test at the wheel of identical MINI Cooper S racers with John Cooper Works Tuning Kit, plus quad biking and karting. After an exciting but sporting battle, Belgium's Maxime Martin took the inaugural world championship title ahead of Fredrik Lestrup (Sweden) and Johannes Stuck (Austria). The only woman in the field, Steffi Halm of Germany, finished in fifth position.

The climax to MINI United was suitably spectacular, with Sunday's Special Guest Race – in which 17

celebrity MINI enthusiasts went head-to-head on the track – topping the bill. Among the stars lining up on the grid were Swiss ex-Formula One driver Marc Surer, Italy's former Touring Car World Champion Roberto Ravaglia, Finnish "rally professor" Rauno Aaltonen, Italian singer Max Gazzè and twice Champ Car champion and former F1 ace Alessandro Zanardi. The Italian, today one of the leading drivers in the FIA World Touring Car Championship, came out on top after a thrilling battle with German MINI CHALLENGE 2004 champion Alexander Burgstaller. "This victory on my tenth wedding anniversary and in front of my home crowd is something very special for me," said the fans' favourite. "Una vittoria speciale" for Zanardi – and "un' esperienza speciale" for around 6,000 fans at MINI United.

(1) Smiles all round at MINI United. (2) The Circuito Santamonica in Misano was the perfect location for the largest ever international MINI get-together. (3) The MINI CHALLENGE drivers had to show their versatility on quad bikes. (4) This Bisazza MINI sported a glistening coating of 30,000 mosaic stones. (5) MINI Classic fans were equally at home in Misano. (6) Dimitri travelled 3,600 kilometres in his MINI to join the enthusiasts at MINI United. (7) The MINI fans were also allowed out onto the track in their own pride and joy.

Facts
& Figures.

The MINI embodies almost
50 years of automotive history. It is a
history full of surprising statistics and
amusing anecdotes, stories great and small,
outstanding and dramatic rally victories,
comical moments and major triumphs.

A kaleidoscope.

MINI wears BISAZZA

— Creations from Italian mosaic specialists BISAZZA represent the ultimate in interior design, and there isn't much you can't decorate with their precious stones. Bathtubs, swimming pools, saunas, the dome of a mosque, a park bench and more than one bar in Milan have all been embellished with BISAZZA mosaics. In 2005, MINI joined the BISAZZA-clad ranks. Designers Carlo dal Bianco and Marco Braga dressed a total of five models, coating each MINI in 37,000 shimmering glass stones (31,700 on the Cabrio / Convertible models). The results are certainly impressive. The joint project between MINI and BISAZZA has produced five customised one-off models highlighting the clear and flawless fusion of fashion and design. Dama, for example, is a successful interpretation of the optical style of the sixties, the captivating Zebra design feeds off the trend for animal-inspired styling and sparks recollections of Africa, while Tartan represents an updated version of the classical "British Style". Other variations that perfectly match the MINI are the Summer Flowers design and the Piet de Poule look. These five outfits allow each MINI to express its individual personality in a most striking way.

MINI Always Open

— The MINI Cabrio / Convertible isn't the first MINI to "go topless". Ever since the early days of the cult car there have been workshops and amateur enthusiasts only too willing to relieve the hatchback of its metal roof. Some even went as far as shortening the wheelbase to create a two-seater roadster. However, the first official convertible MINI Classic wasn't unveiled until 1993. Built in cooperation with German drop-top specialists Karmann, the new cabriolet cost the handsome sum of 12,000 pounds sterling. That secured the first owners of this luxurious MINI Classic a dashboard trimmed in burr walnut, velour-covered bucket seats and a 1,265 cc engine. A strictly limited production run of 414 helped in no small measure to secure the model's exclusive status.

The new MINI Cabrio / Convertible, presented at the Geneva Motor Show in March 2004, was more refined than its predecessors and technically a different animal. The cabriolet was fitted with an electrically operated soft top, complex body reinforcement and twin roll-over bars, adding an extra layer of optimum occupant protection to go with the hallmark MINI fun factor at the wheel and that incomparable open-air feeling. No wonder the MINI Cabrio / Convertible has become a world-beater.

Lessons the kids will love

— For many of us, sitting in the driver's seat and having a just-for-fun twist of the steering wheel is a classic image of childhood. At the Ravensburger Spieleland amusement and theme park in Meckenbeuren-Liebenau near Lake Constance, this time-honoured dry run in Dad's parked car takes on a whole new excitement. Here, youngsters can negotiate their way around a 2,000-square-metre traffic course consisting of roads, traffic lights, pedestrian crossings and signposts. A fleet of 34 faithfully reproduced electric MINI Cooper S single-seaters (pictured) give schoolchildren their first taste of car driving. The kids' driving school begins with a short theory lesson, before the practical section gets underway in the MINI cars. At the end of the course, the kids earn themselves a special driving licence – provided they have shown thoughtfulness and care during their driving test.

Needless to say, there is also a MINI driving course for adults. MINI is offering a MINI Driver Training initiative at its driver centre at Munich airport, in which participants learn how to keep a handle on that high-speed go-kart feeling – even in critical situations.

MINI for very special occasions

— Numerous special editions of the MINI Classic and the new MINI get pulses racing among fans past and present. The first special model was the Mini 1000 Special launched in 1975 with green and white bodywork, Safari floor mats and seat covers in bright orange sunlounger look. This bold combination was a cool look in the seventies. It was followed in the eighties and nineties by the new special models known as Chelsea, Ritz, Piccadilly and Park Lane, evoking famous parts of London, while the Designer special conjured up the sixties fashion scene. And then there was the Mini Advantage in white. The new MINI Cooper has also been available in a special Park Lane edition (pictured above), its distinctive features including special chromed exterior mirrors, striking bonnet stripes and other bodywork decals. The next special editions to be launched were the MINI Seven and the MINI Checkmate with its unmistakable chequered flag design.

From MINI Classic to the podium

— **The son of a well-to-do family was expected to go to university before embarking on a respectable career.** Instead, at the age of 19, Nikolaus Andreas Lauda bought himself a race-trim MINI Classic from Austrian touring car champion Fritz Baumgartner and lined up for his first hillclimb event in Mühllacken near Linz on April 15th, 1968. He duly finished second – behind Baumgartner, as it turned out. Two weeks later, Niki Lauda sped to his first career victory in the Dobratsch hill-climb, throwing his MINI Classic through the hairpins with a bravery unmatched by any of his more experienced rivals.

The rest of Lauda's high-speed story is well documented, the Austrian going on to win three Formula One world championships. The MINI Classic also proved to be the springboard to success for other racing drivers. Indeed, Formula One champions Graham Hill, John Surtees, Jackie Stewart, Jochen Rindt and James Hunt all discovered their talent for quick cornering in the MINI. But it wasn't only the drivers from the sixties, seventies and eighties who enjoyed a quick burn at the wheel of this car. 21st-century Formula One stars like Juan Pablo Montoya and David Coulthard also like to swap their 900 hp racers for a MINI Cooper S in their spare time.

Inspiration for a global hit

— **"Keep on Running", recorded in 1966, was the breakthrough for the Spencer Davis Group.** The band fronted by former German teacher Spencer Davis sealed its place in the rock'n'roll establishment, toured with the Rolling Stones and The Who, and celebrated a dozen or so number one hits over the years.

"Keep on Running" was the first successful record produced by the band, topping the charts in Great Britain and climbing to number eight in Germany. But what has that got to do with MINI?

Legend has it that Davis came up with the lively, impatient sound and almost pleading lyrics for "Keep on Running" in a Mini Cooper.

Davis was apparently driving through the Scottish Highlands at 3.30 in the morning: the thermometer had dipped to three degrees Celsius, a howling gale was battering the car, and thunder and hail had also joined the fray. Looking at the fuel gauge, the only thought in Davis' mind was: keep on running!

City slicker

— **3.69 metres long, 1.68 metres wide and 1.40 metres tall: the MINI is a small car.** With a turning circle of not much more than ten metres and available with a range of highly responsive engines, it is the ideal model for the twists and turns of the urban jungle. And that's far more than just a marketing claim. The MINI really cannot get enough of the big-city buzz and bustle – as a look at MINI hotspots around the world can prove. The top-ten locations around the globe in terms of concentration of MINI cars read like a Who's Who of world cities: London, Los Angeles, Miami, Munich, Berlin, Singapore, New York, Hong Kong, Seoul and Atlanta.

And just to make sure there are no misunderstandings – a genuine MINI also thrives on twisty country roads outside the confines of towns and cities. After all, it is cars and drivers that create a driving style, not the place name on a signpost.

Mini Clubman – a car for those who need to spread out a little

— **The MINI Classic was always more than simply a two-door car.** Over the course of its lifespan it took on the identity of a van, convertible and pick-up, but one of the most popular variants were the Traveller and its close relatives, the Countryman and Clubman. This estate model had a longer chassis and split rear doors, lending it impressive versatility. More than 200,000 units were built between 1960 and 1969.

45 years on from the launch of the original Traveller, MINI unveiled the Concept Frankfurt at the 2005 International Motor Show in Frankfurt. This fresh interpretation of the Traveller was fitted with side doors based on parallelogram kinematics, allowing unimpeded access to the spacious rear seats. At the rear, side-hinged doors help to open up the versatile load area to its full potential.

The surprise package in Frankfurt was followed by variations on the concept car at the motor shows in Tokyo, Detroit and Geneva, giving the public a teasing glimpse of how a future MINI variant could shape up.

On gravel, snow or ice, the MINI Classic was unbeatable

— **With its wheels positioned right in the car's four corners, the MINI Classic soon came to be seen as the perfect rally car, one that could even make life uncomfortable for much larger rivals.** The Rallye Monte Carlo represented the breakthrough for the MINI Classic into the racing scene. In addition to its three victories in this prestigious event, it notched up another ten wins in major international rallies between 1965 and 1967 alone. Rauno Aaltonen was the BMC team's most successful driver, recording a total of eight top-class victories with the Mini Cooper S.

The MINI Classic shows its true mettle

— **The series-produced MINI made its first appearance on British roads in 1959; but little did it know, it already had a more powerful brother in the offing.** Nobody had yet laid eyes on the car in question, which was still little more than a dot on the horizon of John Cooper's imagination.

This car tuner, developer, designer and friend of MINI Classic inventor Sir Alec Issigonis harboured a burning desire to build a prototype. Just how strong this desire had become was demonstrated by the cooperation arrangement he agreed to – one which hardly left him richly rewarded. BMC restricted its financial contribution to a proportion of the development costs and handed Cooper just two pounds sterling for every MINI Classic sold bearing the Cooper badge.

Unveiled in September 1961, the first Mini Cooper was powered by a 997 cc engine developing 55 hp at 6,000 rpm. Hitting a top speed of 140 km/h, it was substantially more agile than the 116 km/h series-produced MINI Classic. The immediate sales success of his first model gave Cooper's creativity fresh impetus and the next version of his car hit the roads in 1963. The motor sport-inspired Mini Cooper S boasted both extra engine displacement (1,071 cc) and power (68 hp). It was therefore no surprise when the first Mini Cooper S powered and drifted its way to its major breakthrough: third and sixth places overall in the 1963 Rallye Monte Carlo. Proving that these performances were no flash in the pan, the Mini Cooper S backed them up by topping the overall classification of this history-laden rally a sensational three times – in 1964, 1965 and 1967. The era of this legendary British car ended prematurely with the 75 hp Cooper 1275 S, in production until 1971. It wasn't until 1990 that the Mini Cooper returned to the scene – as a limited-edition model restricted to 1,000 units.

FACT 11

MINI goes logo

— **The current MINI logo depicts a chrome wheel with stylised wings and the word "MINI" set against a black background in the centre.** The trademark is a 21st-century interpretation of the MINI logo introduced in the mid-1990s.

The historical roots of both logos can be traced back to the late 1940s when Morris adorned its vehicles, like the famous Morris Minor (1948), with a trademark derived from the coat of arms of Lord Nuffield (the official title of company founder William Morris). In the centre of a winged circle or wheel was a red ox standing over three blue waves, the symbol of the City of Oxford.

In 1959 this trademark was introduced in modified form on the first MINI Classic, the Morris Mini-Minor. From 1969, British parent company British Leyland marketed the MINI Classic as a separate brand with its own trademark. The logo they chose for the car, however, was a modern, abstract design bearing absolutely no relation to the Morris trademark used up to then.

It wasn't until 1990 that the company returned to the lines of the old Morris badge, creating a new logo reserved initially for the new edition of the Mini Cooper. In 1996 the logo was introduced on all MINI Classic models, although now with a modified (green) background and new-style MINI lettering.

FACT 12

The next MINI is all lined up

— **A replacement for the original MINI Classic took shape on the drawing boards as early as 1967.** The design created by Sir Alec Issigonis, the technical brains behind the original MINI Classic, produced a prototype with the code name 9X. The aim was to create a car that was smaller, lighter and five percent cheaper to make than the 1959 car.

Unbelievably, the 9X was even four inches (ten centimetres) shorter than its predecessor, yet its small bonnet and greater width allowed extra space inside. Added to which, the new car sported an innovative "semi hatchback" – a folding rear window, which was to prove the precursor to the bootlid of the new MINI.

Two prototypes were built, but the project never reached fruition after British Leyland took over production of the MINI Classic in 1968. The new owners had no interest in investing in such a radical project. Fortunately, Issigonis disregarded the management's orders and kept the prototypes safely stored away. Today, a 9X is one of the exhibits on display in the Heritage Motor Centre in Gaydon, England.

FACT 13

MINI Classic challenges "bubble cars"

— **The original MINI Classic was born out of the potential fallout from the Suez Crisis of 1956 and the looming breakdown of oil deliveries from the Middle East.** The chairman of the British Motor Corporation (BMC), Sir Leonard Lord, feared that a disruption of fuel supplies would result in a rise in sales figures of micro cars from Italy and Germany. One such model was the Isetta, which was produced – ironically enough – by BMW Group.

The Isetta had a front-hinged door and a maximum speed of 85 km/h, but it also boasted rock-bottom fuel consumption of barely four litres of petrol over 100 kilometres (around 60 mpg).

Lord gave the go-ahead for the development of the ADO15 (ADO was an acronym for the Austin Drawing Office) Mini in 1957. He insisted on using an existing BMC powerplant for the car, but was otherwise happy to let his brilliant chief designer Alec Issigonis give full vent to his vast reserves of creativity.

FACT 14

A Ferrari or a MINI Classic?

— **The Beatles, Steve McQueen and Twiggy were not the only celebrity owners of a MINI Classic.** In the 1960s, visitors to the Ferrari factory in Maranello, Italy, were greeted by the rather surprising sight of a Mini Cooper – belonging to none other than company director Enzo Ferrari.

Witnesses claim that the legendary "Commendatore" regularly used to relax with a drive in the mountains at the wheel of his MINI Classic.

The MINI remains hugely popular among racing drivers today, with Formula One star David Coulthard just one of many famous MINI fans.

FACT 15
MINI goes to Hollywood

— No film has defined the quintessential characteristics of the MINI more effectively than *The Italian Job*. The original version of 1968 was set in Italy, the Mini Cooper taking on a starring role as a getaway car after a gold robbery.

The movie took on cult status in Great Britain and the line: "You were only supposed to blow the bloody doors off!" passed into cinematic legend. Amazingly, the main star of the film – Michael Caine – only learnt to drive in the 1980s. A Hollywood remake of *The Italian Job* was filmed in 2003, with

Mark Wahlberg and Charlize Theron in the headline roles. In homage to the original movie, the action begins in Venice, but soon switches scenery to Los Angeles, where the MINI Cooper S plays a glittering role. Three MINI models are recruited by the crooks to transport their plundered gold bars. Cinema audiences were gripped as the MINI tore through traffic, nailed spectacular jumps and even escaped through the entrance to the subway on the famous Hollywood Boulevard.

FACT 16
MINI made to measure

— Each and every MINI consists of some 3,000 components, and no two MINI cars are ever the same. Every MINI is built to order and each car bears a unique "build label".

If the customer has specified a satellite navigation system, a Harman-Kardon stereo system and leather trim, for example, these details are logged specifically in the label's barcode. A total of 256 different robots and 4,500 associates join forces to create each MINI, with 3,800 spot welds required to build each bodyshell. Every robot works to a tolerance of 0.05 millimetres – that's half the width of a human hair.

FACT 17
MINI twins are statistically rare

— **The MINI can be ordered with a limitless range of trim and equipment combinations.** Customers can choose anything from Mellow Yellow with black bonnet stripes, Oxygen Blue with a white roof or a Union Jack roof, diesel or petrol, all the way to the sporty variant of the MINI Cooper S with John Cooper Works Tuning Kit. There's hardly one MINI like another. MINI fans can choose from twelve exterior colours – including eight metallic paint finishes – and roof colours in white, black or body colour. And there are no limits to the number of interior design variations, either. Trim is available in six different variants – from sporty aluminium to classical wood, with matching upholstery in fabric, leather or a fabric/leather combination. But that's not all: the steering wheel and gearshift lever can also be kitted out to the owner's personal tastes. It's no wonder that, for every 100,000 MINI models rolling off the production line at the MINI plant in Oxford, you'll rarely find two the same.

FACT 18
MINI on the lookout for shooting stars

— *MINIInternational*, **the MINI lifestyle magazine, explores cities on the move, unearths trends and talks to creative movers and shakers from the worlds of film, fashion, music, media, art and literature.** Prize-winning art directors and photographers lend each issue a fresh design, which reflects the spirit and soul of the featured city. *MINIInternational* is also looking to promote young talent. To this end, it launched the MINIInternational Photo Award in 2005. The prize is presented every year as part of the International Talent Support (ITS)

initiative, one of the most important international festivals for young fashion and accessory designers. In 2006 Remigiusz Pyrdol (pictured here) persuaded the judges with his creative photo series on the theme of emigration.

The MINIInternational Photo Award is geared towards students from the world's leading photography schools and is presented each summer in a ceremony in the Italian port of Trieste. The works submitted by the candidates are assessed by a panel of judges made up of a Who's Who of globally renowned art directors, curators, deputy editors and photographers, who judge the entrants according to both creativity and technical quality. But the jury's main job stretches beyond just presenting a certificate and prize money: this award is intended to help creative young talent to negotiate the tricky step up to full-time employment. In addition to the prize money, the winner is therefore also commissioned to produce the photos for a city featured in one of the four issues of *MINIInternational* published each year.

MINI Classic – the symbol of a generation

— Although the MINI Classic cost only 496 pounds sterling including taxes at its presentation on August 26th, 1959, sales got off to a sluggish start. However, by 1962 annual production had already reached 200,000 cars and remained consistently above this mark until 1977. With artists, musicians, designers and movie stars falling for the charms of the MINI Classic as the perfect city car, it became a symbol for an entire generation. Production of the MINI Classic hit the one-million mark as early as 1965.

Four years later, there were two million MINI Classics on the world's roads, and that number swelled to three million by 1972 and four million in 1976. The five-millionth MINI Classic left the factory in 1986 and over 5.3 million units had been built by the time production was wrapped up in 2000. If you parked all these cars in a line, the MINI Classic would create a 17,000-kilometre traffic jam stretching from London to Sydney.

MINI travels the globe

— The last MINI Classic rolled off the assembly line at the Longbridge factory in England in October 2000, bringing to an end a production run lasting 41 years. In 1994, BMW Group bought out the British Rover Group, and a year later came the decision to create a whole new generation of the MINI. Bernd Pischetsrieder, Chairman of BMW Group and the new man in charge of Rover, announced to British magazine *Car* at the time: "Our plan is to build a new car that will be a trendsetter and embody radical innovation in the same way as the MINI Classic. And that's not going to be easy."

BMW gave the public a glimpse of the newly developed car in September 1997, although it had to wait until the Paris Motor Show in October 2000 for its official presentation. Series production began at the new factory in Oxford in April 2001, with sales getting underway in Great Britain that July, across Europe in September 2001 and in America in the spring of 2002. The MINI is now enjoying considerable success in more than 75 countries around the world.

A glimpse of the future: the ACV 30

— To mark the 30th anniversary of the MINI triumph in the Rallye Monte Carlo, Rover unveiled a design concept in 1997 that already embodied elements of the future MINI. Yet this development was still very much rooted in retro with its 16-inch wheels, gleaming chrome radiator grille and button indicators that harked back to the 1960s, as well as its round headlamps. New design territory was broached with doors that extended high into the roof and powerfully flared wheel arches. A large tailgate also distinguished the futuristic, 3.5-metre-long car from the MINI Classic production model. The design study went by the name of Anniversary Concept Vehicle (ACV 30) and was based on the MGF roadster chassis, featuring the same mid-engine with 1.8 litres displacement and an output of 120 hp.

High birth rate at MINI Plant Oxford

— **Legend has it that the MINI Classic was conceived on the hallowed ground of the MINI plant in Oxford.** Production of the MINI Classic began at what was then known as the Cowley plant in 1959, and cars have been built there ever since.

Today, the factory stretches out over an area of 453,248 square metres, and in 2005 production of the MINI totalled 200,119 units. BMW Group invested an initial 280 million pounds to ensure that the factory was packed with the best production equipment any-where in the world. Another 100 million have recently been ploughed into the bodyshop and paintshop in order to meet demand. More than 4,500 people, known as "associates", are employed at the Oxford plant, which also welcomes more than 14,000 visitors a year. "The people who work here don't talk about building a car," says John Thomas, who takes groups of visitors on tours of the factory. "We call it 'giving birth to a MINI'."

It's small, but it makes a big impression

— **By definition a MINI has to be small, but it must also meet the demands of modern engine technology and respond to changes in the world in which it operates.** For example, the average adult nowadays is significantly larger than in the 1950s. Safety in cars has changed beyond all recognition over the past 50 years, while customers now also expect better performance and rather more in the way of luxury. Mirrors and windows are now electrically operated, as is the air conditioning system. And it's hard to picture life at the wheel without a high-quality stereo and satellite navigation.

Under these circumstances, it was inevitable that the MINI would be an altogether larger car than the MINI Classic. Indeed, the 21st-century model is 57 centimetres longer than the original and has 45 percent more volume. But the car's classical proportions, with a short bonnet and the wheels right in the corners, has been retained, ensuring that the MINI is and will remain a MINI.

MINI for all the senses

— **See, hear, taste, smell, feel – at the world's first MINI LOUNGE, which opened its doors in Madrid in 2005, guests could experience the MINI with all their senses.** The tasteful décor and extraordinary light effects inside this unique combination of bar, lounge and restaurant reflect MINI lifestyle characteristics and are complemented by a live DJ and a special party at weekends.

In addition to a restaurant area, the 270-square-metre lounge also features a seventies-style chill-out area. The bar is adorned with the glass stones of Bisazza's hallmark black and white design, and even the toilets are decked out in a wild animal style.

Red hot

— **"Is it love?" asked the slogan for the relaunch of the MINI. And hundreds of thousands answered yes, ja, si or oui.** No wonder the love that owners feel for their MINI is also expressed in their favourite colours. The global favourite when it comes to paint shades is the powerful Chili Red: after all, red is the colour of love, passion and desire.

Second in the MINI colour popularity stakes is Pepper White, presumably the choice primarily of purists, aesthetes, iPod fans and those owners never happier than when giving their MINI a good scrub.

Was your favourite MINI colour one of those in the MINI (2001-2006) list? The top ten was completed, in the following order, by Pure Silver, Astro Black, Black, Hyper Blue, Electric Blue, British Racing Green, Dark Silver and, finally, Black Eye Purple.

Technical Features.

ABS

The MINI features the latest-generation Anti-lock Braking System (ABS) with sensor-controlled Electronic Brakeforce Distribution.

AMBIENT LIGHTING

Switch colour lighting illuminates the instrument panel, the B-pillars, the door stowage areas and the door openers.

AIRBAGS

Driver and passenger airbags are part of the standard equipment on current MINI models. The driver airbag is in the steering wheel, the passenger airbag is in the dashboard. Both are so-called intelligent airbags which inflate according to the severity of the impact. If a child seat is attached to the passenger seat, the passenger airbag can be switched off via a key switch on the passenger side. This is indicated by a telltale light in the roof module.

Two side airbags are also part of the standard features of every MINI. They are concealed in the outer upholstery of the left and right front seatbacks, providing extremely effective protection against injury to the thorax and stomach of the driver and front passenger.

Apart from the driver, passenger and side airbags, the current R56 models also feature curtain head airbags as standard. They are located in the roof lining directly above the windows. If deployed in an impact, these bolster-type airbags cover the front and rear side windows like a curtain, protecting front and rear occupants not only against impacts but also against glass splinters.

AUTOMATIC STABILITY CONTROL PLUS TRACTION (ASC+T)

A standard feature on the MINI Cooper S and MINI Cooper S Cabrio / Convertible, Automatic Stability Control + Traction (ASC+T) gives the driver the sense of "sticking" to the road. This system is optionally available for all the other MINI models. It prevents the wheels from spinning when engine torque is applied. This is particularly beneficial when MINI drivers accelerate from standstill on a slippery road surface or when pulling out into fast-moving traffic.

ASC+T ensures optimum traction and directional stability. It prevents wheelspin by applying brake force to the relevant wheel. To prevent both wheels from spinning, engine torque is reduced.

AUTOMATIC TRANSMISSION

The optional six-speed automatic transmission on the current MINI Cooper, MINI Cooper S and MINI Cooper S Cabrio / Convertible injects an extra dose of go-kart feeling and driving fun. The perfect timing of the automatic gear changes within a fraction of a second lets you get the absolute maximum out of the engine when accelerating.

Drivers can choose whether to leave gear changes entirely to the automatic transmission or use the switch paddles on the steering wheel to initiate gear shifts themselves. Even when accelerating at relatively low speeds, the torque converter guarantees a direct, rigid connection to the engine for a nippy ride both in urban traffic and out on the open road. Thanks to Adaptive Transmission Control (ATC), rising or falling gradients are effortlessly overcome. ATC

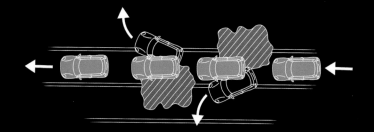

Automatic Stability Control + Traction (ASC +T) **prevents the driven front wheels from spinning to ensure optimal start-up and safe traction.**

instantly responds to any uphill or downhill slopes, automatically shifting down in response to changes in speed and pressure on the accelerator pedal. The automatic transmission also has a built-in safety feature: not only does it check whether manual gear changes are appropriate, it will also prevent any gear changes in critical situations when the optional DSC system is activated.

B

BRAKES

As the most powerful member of the MINI model range, the new MINI Cooper S comes with the most powerful brakes. It is fitted with standard 16-inch brakes (disc size: 294 mm x 22 mm) on the front axle. They guarantee excellent stopping performance, outstanding grip and very short braking distances. The front brake discs of the MINI are inner-vented. The MINI brakes allow for outstanding deceleration values and short stopping distances. The brake system of the MINI is designed to endure even frequent and intense use with virtually no signs of wear such as brake judder or fading. Control systems such as Electronic Brakeforce Distribution (EBD) and Cornering Brake Control (CBC) also contribute to the first-rate braking characteristics of the MINI. The new MINI features a Brake Assistant as standard.

C

CONTRAST ROOF

The contrast roof is one of the striking distinguishing features of the MINI. It already marked out the MINI Classic of the sixties and even today it makes every MINI Cooper and MINI Cooper S a very special car. Depending on the body colour, both models can have a black or white roof and exterior mirrors in the relevant colour. If the roof is painted white, the alloy wheels can also be ordered in white at no extra cost. Naturally, every model can also feature a roof in the body colour at no extra charge.

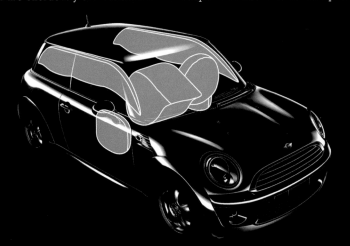

The driver and front passenger airbags protect **the head and chest in the event of a frontal collision.** Side airbags **reduce the risk of injury in the hip and thorax area, while the** curtain head airbags **provide effective protection against head injury in a side-on collision.**

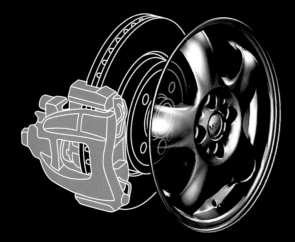

The four disc brakes feature as standard the Anti-lock Braking System (ABS), Cornering Brake Control (CBC) and Electronic Brakeforce Distribution (EBD).

CORNERING BRAKE CONTROL (CBC)

The Cornering Brake Control (CBC) system is governed by the ABS control unit and uses the same slip detection system. CBC calculates transverse acceleration on bends and ensures that optimum brakeforce is applied to each wheel. This ensures that the MINI is always kept under control – regardless of road conditions or the weight of the load being carried.

Unlike DSC, CBC will only come into effect when the brakes are applied.

CRASH TEST RESULTS

The new MINI offers a wide range of features for passive safety in every respect. The new MINI fulfils legal requirements in all countries in which it is marketed. And it naturally offers all the prerequisites for optimum results in all crash tests relevant the world over:
- use of extremely stable load-bearing structures and an extremely rigid occupant compartment
- highly efficient restraint systems
- intelligent deformation pathways, which channel energy in the event of a collision
- standard airbag system comprising no fewer than six airbags.
This ensures optimum protection for MINI occupants.

D

DAB

The current MINI is the only car in its segment to allow for digital radio reception in Europe. Thanks to the DAB tuner, MINI drivers can enjoy crystal-clear reception. Moreover, using these digital signals many extra services can be called up, such as the name of the music currently playing, the performer, genre etc. In areas where there is no digital signal, the system automatically switches to analogue reception.
To receive digital radio stations, the Radio Boost CD or navigation system has to be installed.

DIRECT FUEL INJECTION

The power units for the latest MINI are the benchmark for the compact class. A turbo engine with direct fuel injection lends the MINI even more dynamics and agility. At the same time, fuel consumption and emission levels have been significantly reduced compared with the predecessor model.

DYNAMIC STABILITY CONTROL (DSC)

Using ABS and other sensors, Dynamic Stability Control measures brake cylinder pressure and the angle of the steering wheel, as well as monitoring whether the car is rotating about its own axis (commonly known as "yaw"). It will then vary the brake pressure on individual wheels and adjust the engine torque via the powertrain controller.

This helps to rectify any instability that may be caused by sharp acceleration or braking, tight corners or sudden load changes. It also reduces the risk of oversteer and understeer.

Dynamic Stability Control is available on all MINI models and comprises all upstream control systems such as ABS, ASC+T and Hill Assist. By using numerous sensors, DSC recognises critical driving situations and responds in a split second by intervening in the engine management or by dispensing the appropriate brakeforce to the wheels. For example, the system is able to apply the brakes to individual wheels. Skidding, oversteer and understeer are recognised at the outset and prevented as far as is physically possible, ensuring optimum ride stability and safety. Thanks to the instant pick-up and transmission of data, DSC can also respond significantly faster to dangerous situations than a driver ever could. Even so, MINI passengers will hardly notice DSC control in action.

E

EASY LOAD SYSTEM

The Easy Load system of the MINI Cabrio / Convertible is both ingenious and simple. When the soft top is closed, the two levers in the boot can be turned so that the back section of the soft top folds upwards and locks in place for easy loading and unloading.

The boot has a capacity of 165 litres with the soft top closed, and 120 litres with the roof down. This can be almost quadrupled to 605 litres when the soft top is closed and the rear seats are folded down.

ELECTRONIC BRAKEFORCE DISTRIBUTION (EBD)

Electronic Brakeforce Distribution, which is a standard feature in the MINI, controls the brake spread between the front and rear wheels, which may otherwise differ according to the weight being carried by the MINI.

If the MINI has a heavy rear load (passengers, fuel and luggage),

In the event of an accident, the doors are automatically unlocked and the hazard warning flashers and interior lights are switched on.

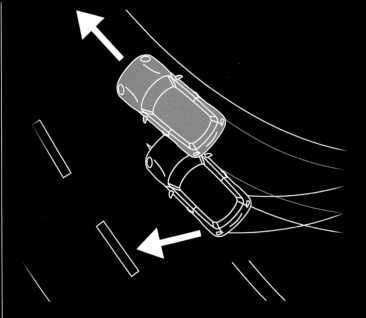

Dynamic Stability Control (DSC) **prevents unstable driving conditions by intervening in the engine management and applying brake pressure to individual wheels.**

the point at which the rear wheels start to lock under braking will correspond approximately with that of the front wheels. Thus a high amount of rear brake force can be applied safely and the vehicle's braking performance is optimised. However, if a MINI not fitted with EBD were carrying a lighter load, the rear wheels would lock before the front wheels, causing a loss of directional stability. EBD distributes the brakeforce in such a way that both sets of brakes achieve optimum effect. The system ensures that the braking distance is as short as possible and also prevents ABS from being activated prematurely.

ENGINE

Since its initial year of production, the MINI has rated as an extremely sporty and agile vehicle, not least thanks to its outstanding driveline concept. To sharpen its edge even further in this crucial area, the current MINI lines up with some all-new engines and a six-speed manual gearbox as standard.

The MINI One and MINI Cooper are the first vehicles in their class to benefit from a normally aspirated engine with fully variable valve control. Drivers of the MINI Cooper S can depend on their high-performance turbo unit with direct fuel injection to deliver the power. And with the overboost function and six-speed manual transmission, the MINI scales new heights in terms of driving dynamics and agility. Beyond this, numerous other features such as a volume flow-controlled oil pump and on-demand water pump ensure that the MINI will remain among the most reliable and environmentally compatible vehicles in its class in the future as well.

EQUAL LENGTH DRIVE SHAFTS

In most small cars with front-wheel drive and a transversely mounted engine the gearbox is positioned off-centre. This imbalance results in axle shafts of differing length on the left and right. As the feedback effect on corners is greater on the shorter axle side, there is a general feeling of instability when driving.

The MINI, however, gets the balance perfect: the axle contains an additional driveshaft bearing which compensates for the different lengths. This optimisation eliminates torque steer and guarantees an all-round feeling of safety behind the wheel.

F

FULLY VARIABLE VALVE CONTROL

The current MINI Cooper is the first vehicle in the small and compact car segment to feature a naturally aspirated engine with fully variable valve train. The engine of the MINI Cooper develops 120 hp/88 kW from a displacement of 1.6 litres.

The valve train is modelled on the BMW Valvetronic system. Unlike conventional engines, an engine with fully variable valve control regulates the engine power not by means of a throttle valve but by continuously varying the valve lift and the opening times of the intake valves. If the driver goes easy on the accelerator, valve lift is reduced. Under harder acceleration, the amount of valve lift is increased. Thus the fuel/air mixture in the cylinder can be adjusted for all driving situations. Fully variable valve control has several advantages. Firstly it reduces emissions and fuel consumption, depending on topography, by up to 20 percent. At the same time, due to an optimised combustion process, the engine is also more responsive, thereby enhancing the typical sporty driving character of the MINI.

H

HEATED FRONT WINDSCREEN

Scraping away ice on bitterly cold winter days is a thing of the past thanks to the heated front windscreen. Available as an option for all MINI models, it contains minute heating elements (virtually invisible to the naked eye) which are embedded in the front screen approximately 1 cm apart and function in the same way as for the rear windscreen heating.

The heated front windscreen is timed to operate in accordance with the outside temperature.

HILL ASSIST

The Hill Assist function in the current MINI is part of the DSC (Dynamic Stability Control) system. It automatically prevents roll-back on inclines, thus significantly facilitating moving off on a gradient. If DSC's tilt sensors recognise that the car is at an angle, the brake pressure to keep the MINI in place is automatically provided. As soon as the driver wants to move off again and enough torque has been developed to pull away safely, the brake is automatically released. This function is deactivated as soon as the handbrake is applied or if the driver moves the car within a short time of releasing the brake pedal.

I

IMMOBILISER

The immobiliser, standard on all MINI models, is controlled by the vehicle electronics system. It prevents hotwiring and is enabled as soon as the key is removed from the slot or as soon as the coded fob is removed from the vehicle.

INTERIOR LIGHTS

The illumination pack includes lighting in the door trim, reading lights at the front, illuminated vanity mirrors, footwell lights at the front and lights in the centre of the rooflining. Switch colour lighting illuminates the instrument panel, the B-pillars, the door stowage areas and the door openers.

ISOFIX CHILD SEAT ATTACHMENTS

With the ISOFIX child seat attachments, even the most restless infant will be sitting snugly and securely in the back of the MINI. The MINI child seats, which are available in a range of sizes, can be anchored to the body of the MINI via mounting bars integrated into the rear seats.

K

KEY MEMORY / KEY READER

At first glance the MINI ignition key appears to be ... well, a key. In fact, it is a portable data archive.

This intelligent door-unlocker can store basic data such as the chassis number, mileage and service interval status. When you take your MINI in for a service, all you have to do is hand over your key containing all the relevant vehicle data.

With the Key Reader, the MINI dealer can simply retrieve all the data required and take care of things. The MINI remote key and coded fob features a remote control that allows the doors, tailgate and fuel tank lid of the MINI to be unlocked and locked from a distance.

L

LIMITED SLIP DIFFERENTIAL

Optionally available for the MINI Cooper S, the Limited Slip Differential prevents power being drained away at a spinning wheel by transferring torque to the drive wheel with most grip. The MINI Cooper S is therefore always able to make the most of the available engine power, and can accelerate more quickly out of bends. The improved dynamics are particularly noticeable on winding or serpentine roads.

As well as allowing a sportier driving style, the Limited Slip Differential also provides improved stability and safety on split-friction surfaces.

M

MCPHERSON FRONT AXLE

The front axle of the MINI is constructed according to the space-saving McPherson principle. This involves a coil spring being wrapped around a shock absorber acting as an upper control arm, all combined in a single unit.

Unlike on most vehicles in the small-car segment, the front suspension of the MINI has two precise steel bearings instead of rubber joints attached to the engine block. This optimises the front wheel location as well as improving performance when speeding up, slowing down or tackling corners.

MULTIFUNCTION STEERING WHEEL

With the man comfort features offered by the multifunction steering wheel, drivers can keep their attention focused firmly on the road ahead. In addition to the cruise control system, the multifunction steering wheel also has combined switches which allow drivers to switch

between the audio modes (tuner, cassette, CD) as well as adjust the volume and search for the next radio station or CD track. It also enables operation of the voice control system and the mobile phone interface.

MULTILINK REAR SUSPENSION

The multilink rear supension of the MINI is absolutely unique in the small-car segment. Initially developed for a rear-wheel drive car, it has been tailored perfectly to suit the front-wheel drive, weight distribution and handling of the MINI. The wheels of the MINI are always in full contact with the road surface, ensuring optimimum steering response and traction regardless of the bumpiness of the road surface. Its long, straight longitudinal members also help to enhance the rear stability of the MINI in the event of a collision.

N

NAVIGATION SYSTEM

The navigation system in the MINI will show you where to go – any-

where in the world and to an accuracy of approx. five metres.

The Global Positioning System (GPS) is always linked to at least three satellites, which ensures that the navigation system can be used in the most remote parts of the world. The updatable map DVD contains street information for the country in question. The system provides drivers with audible and visual information on the best route, including details of approaching junctions and useful facilities and landmarks along the way. A built-in gyrocompass determines the direction, while speed pulses are received from the ABS system.

O

OVERBOOST

The new overboost function of the current MINI Cooper S allows for a sporty driving style and fast overtaking. From second gear upwards, sensors pick up hard acceleration, prompting the overboost function to increase the charge pressure by 150 mbar in a speed range between 1700 and 4500 rpm.
This raises torque from 240 to a maximum 260 Nm for a significant increase in agility. Compared to the previous model, for example, the new MINI Cooper S shaves 2.5 s off the 80 to 120 km/h acceleration time in sixth gear.

The overboost function thus guarantees greater dynamics as well as more agile and lively handling. This avoids a higher rated output and with it a less favourable insurance class.

P

PARK DISTANCE CONTROL (PDC)

Park Distance Control (PDC) is part

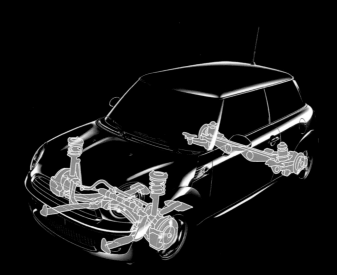

The spring strut front axle based on the McPherson principle **combined with the multilink rear axle ensures optimal handling.**

of the standard equipment of the MINI Cabrio / Convertible and is an option on all other MINI models. It enables you to wriggle into the tiniest of parking spaces without the risk of any scrapes and scratches.

PDC comprises four sensors on the rear bumper and an acoustic transmitter located in the luggage compartment. It is automatically activated one second after reverse gear has been engaged. When the system detects an object, it emits a series of acoustic signals that increase in frequency as the MINI reverses nearer to the obstacle. Once the MINI is within 20 cm of the obstacle, the signal become continuous, warning the driver of the imminent risk of a collision. In conjunction with a navigation system, PDC also assists parking by means of visual information in the current MINI.

R

RAIN SENSOR
The rain sensor detects the amount of rainfall and automatically controls the wiper operating interval accordingly. This is of particular benefit in unpredictable weather conditions or when overtaking on a wet surface.

The sensor uses infra-red light beams to measure the amount of light reflected from the outer surface of the screen. The wiper is automatically activated as soon as rainfall is detected, the wipe rate depending on the wetness of the windscreen and the amount of rainfall.

The rain sensor is mounted against the windscreen immediately behind the rear-view mirror. A heating element keeps the sensor's operating area free of condensation and ice.

RUNFLAT SYSTEM COMPONENT TYRES
Runflat System Component (RSC) tyres are unique in the small-car segment and enable you to drive for a further 150 km (at a maximum speed of 80 km/h) even with a puncture.

Any change in tyre pressure is shown by the Runflat Indicator.

The secret of these impressive properties of the RSC tyres lies in their reinforced tyre walls with insert strips, an extended hump rim and heat-resistant rubber that prevents the tyre walls from collapsing if the tyre pressure drops. ABS, ASC+T and DSC will all continue to function normally in the case of a flat tyre. All 16-inch and 17-inch wheels come with RSC tyres as standard.

S

SAFETY BODYSHELL
The MINI body incorporates numerous advanced safety features for maximum occupant protection. These include:
- high torsional stiffness
- highly resilient structural components which prevent deformation of the passenger cell in the event of an accident
- excellent side impact protection
- vibration damping in the area of the front axle and engine mounts
- use of impact-absorbing materials in the area of the instrument panel, roof pillars and safety steering column
- reinforced door sill panels, reinforced A-pillars (in the MINI Cabrio / Convertible) and B-pillars.

The reinforced sidewalls of the runflat tyres allow you to continue driving at up to 80 km/h even when a tyre has lost all air pressure.

SAFETY STEERING COLUMN
The safety steering column in the MINI incorporates an integrated crash element which prevents the steering column intruding into the passenger cell in an accident. In the event of an impact, a deformation zone reduces the length of the steering column by up to 100 millimetres, thus minimising injuries – particularly in the chest area. In conjunction with the airbag system, this provides optimal protection for MINI drivers. A further reduction in injury risk is provided by the electric steering lock, since a mechanical steering lock which could potentially be struck by the driver's knee is no longer necessary. On current MINI models the steering column is adjustable for both height and reach.

SPORT BUTTON
A press of the Sport button instantly sharpens the responses of the current MINI models. It is optionally available for all models and is situated in front of the gearshift. One of the results of activating the Sport mode is more responsive acceleration. The modified accelerator curve results in a more direct response to even relatively light pressure on the accelerator pedal. At the same time the Sport button also results in a more direct steering ratio and thus sportier steering characteristics. On MINI models equipped with automatic transmission, the transmission too becomes more responsive, with gear changes being performed up to 0.5 seconds more quickly than in "D" mode. Switching off the engine automatically deactivates the Sport button.

START/STOP BUTTON
The Start/Stop button for the current MINI allows the engine to be started at the press of a button. The driver simply inserts the key in the slot, depresses the clutch and brake, presses the Start/Stop button and the engine springs to life immediately. A single press of the button can also be used to shut the engine down.

The driver then presses on the key to release the ignition lock and remove the key.

On vehicles with the optional Comfort Access system, it is not even

necessary to insert the coded fob into the slot. As long as drivers are carrying the fob with them, they can start the car simply by pressing the Start/Stop button.

STEPTRONIC
In Steptronic mode the automatic transmission becomes a semi-automatic. It automatically changes up before the engine reaches maximum revs even if the driver forgets to engage a higher gear. Or if engine speed drops too low, the transmission automatically shifts down one gear.

Any requested downshifts that would result in overrevving are not executed. Rocker switches situated in front of, behind and on either side of the steering wheel produce something of a motor sport feel when changing gear. They allow drivers to change gear while still keeping their hands on the wheel.

SUNROOF
Available for all MINI hatchback models, the large sliding and tilting glass sunroof in the MINI consists of two glass panels. The front panel can be tilted electrically or slid back across the rear panel. Two manually adjustable mesh blinds, which retract to the housing between the two sections, provide protection from excess exposure to the sun. And when it comes to stability, the sunroof is clearly on top as well. Despite the size of the sunroof, the body is as

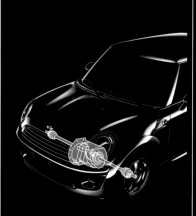

The Limited Slip Differential transfers torque to the drive wheel with grip, thus preventing wheel spin.

stable as in the MINI with a fixed roof. This is due to a reinforcement ring which runs around the sunroof and is welded to the body. In addition, the entire roof construction is so flat that it hardly impairs interior head space at all. The current MINI also features a tilt function on the rear section of the glass sliding roof.

SUPERCHARGER
Until the arrival of the 2006 range, the MINI Cooper S and the MINI Cooper S Cabrio / Convertible were the only cars in their class to offer the benefits of a supercharger. The supercharger is connected directly to the crankshaft, allowing it to provide even power delivery at any engine speed. During the compression process, which takes place inside the supercharger, the intake air is heated to high temperatures, causing it to expand and become thinner. With every piston stroke, less oxygen is pushed into the cylinders. This reduces combustion efficiency and stops the fuel from being used to its full potential. An intercooler counteracts this process by cooling the hot air in the supercharger before it

reaches the combustion chambers. The volume of the air decreases, its density and oxygen content rise and the fuel is burned more efficiently. The intercooler is located above the engine and is fed with fresh air by the eye-catching air scoop on the bonnet.

T

TUNING
The tuning kit specially developed by John Cooper Works for the MINI Cooper S and MINI Cooper S Cabrio / Convertible gives the MINI an even sportier edge.

This kit was developed and tested using the state-of-the-art technology and equipment of one of the world's leading engineering workshops. It gives the MINI more power, more speed and more acceleration.

The JCW tuning kit comprises an optimised cylinder head, modifi-

cations to the air filter system, exhaust system and engine tuning, and supercharging.

TWIN SCROLL TURBOCHARGER
The current MINI Cooper S is the first vehicle in its class to be fitted with a twin-scroll turbocharger.

This means that from each pair of cylinders, the exhaust is fed in two separate ducts to the exhaust manifold and turbocharger, thus reducing exhaust back-pressure and helping the twin-scroll turbocharger to start developing boost at just 1600 rpm. This almost completely eliminates the turbolag effect common on conventionally turbocharged engines. At the same time, torque build-up is as rapid as on a supercharged engine. MINI drivers see the benefits of this increased performance and responsiveness in the form of significantly improved acceleration and reduced fuel consumption.

In order to prevent an excessive build-up of heat in the oil- and water-cooled turbocharger, an electric auxiliary water pump starts up automatically when the engine has been switched off. This quickly dissipates any excess heat from the system.

The reinforced body ensures high torsional stiffness, an extremely strong passenger compartment, impressive ride and acoustic comfort, and optimum protection.

MINI Cooper

ENGINE
Cylinders/arrangement/valves: 4/in-line/4
Displacement: 1598 cc
Stroke/bore: 85.8 / 77.0 mm
Rated output/rated engine speed: 88 kW / 120 hp / 6000 rpm.
Max. torque at engine speed: 160 Nm / 4250 rpm.
Compression ratio/recommended fuel grade: 11.0 / 91-98 RON

TRANSMISSION
Standard transmission ratios:

I/II	:1	13.992 / 7.799
III/IV	:1	5.194 / 3.980
V/VI/R	:1	3.412 / 2.973 / 13.681
Final drive	:1	4.353

PERFORMANCE
Top speed: 203 km/h
Acceleration 0-100 km/h: 9.1 s
In-gear acceleration 80-120 km/h (IV/V/VI): 9.4 / 12.1 / 14.3 s

FUEL CONSUMPTION
Urban: 7.8 l/100 km
Extra-urban: 4.6 l/100 km
Combined: 5.8 l/100 km
CO_2 emissions: 139 g/km
Tank capacity: approx. 40 l

WEIGHT
Kerb weight EU: 1140 kg
Permissible GVW: 1515 kg
Payload capacity: 450 kg
Max. permissible axle load front/rear: 855/740 kg
Towing capacity (trailer with brakes) up to a gradient of 12%: 750 kg
Max. roof load: 75 kg

Length/width/height (mm): 3699 / 1683 / 1407
Wheelbase (mm): 2467

WHEELS
Tyre size front/rear: 175/65 R 15 H
Wheel size front/rear: 5.5 J x 15 LM
Rim type: alloy

ELECTRICS
Battery capacity/installation: 46 AH/front
Alternator capacity: 120 A, 1680 W

MINI Cooper S

ENGINE
Cylinders/arrangement/valves: 4/in-line/4
Displacement: 1598 cc
Stroke/bore: 85.8 / 77.0 mm
Rated output/rated engine speed: 128 kW / 175 hp / 5500 rpm.
Max. torque at engine speed: 240 Nm / 1600 - 5000 rpm.
Compression ratio/recommended fuel grade: 10.5 / 91-98 RON

TRANSMISSION
Standard transmission ratios:

I/II	:1	12.063 / 7.770
III/IV	:1	5.408 / 4.154
V/VI/R	:1	3.460 / 2.975 / 11.783
Final drive	:1	3.647

PERFORMANCE
Top speed: 225 km/h
Acceleration 0-100 km/h: 7.1 s
In-gear acceleration: 80-120 km/h (IV/V/VI): 5.5 / 7.0 / 8.0 s

FUEL CONSUMPTION
Urban: 8.9 l/100 km
Extra-urban: 5.7 l/100 km
Combined: 6.9 l/100 km
CO_2 emissions: 164 g/km
Tank capacity: approx. 50 l

WEIGHT
Kerb weight EU: 1205 kg
Permissible GVW: 1580 kg
Payload capacity: 450 kg
Max. permissible axle load front/rear: 855/755 kg
Towing capacity (trailer with brakes) up to a gradient of 12%: -
Max. roof load: 75 kg

Length/width/height (mm): 3714 / 1683 / 1407
Wheelbase (mm): 2467

WHEELS
Tyre size front/rear: 195/55 R 16 87V RSC
Wheel size front/rear: 6.5 J x 16 LM
Rim type: alloy

ELECTRICS
Battery capacity/installation: 46 AH/front
Alternator capacity: 120 A, 1680 W

MINI One

ENGINE
Cylinders/arrangement/valves: 4/in-line/4
Displacement: 1598 cc
Stroke/bore: 85.8 / 77 mm
Rated output/rated engine speed: 66 kW / 90 hp / 5500 rpm.
Max. torque at engine speed: 140 Nm / 3000 rpm.
Compression ratio/recommended fuel grade: 10.6 / 91-98 RON

TRANSMISSION
Standard transmission ratios:

I/II	:1	13.76 / 7.95
III/IV	:1	5.23 / 3.92
V/VI/R	:1	3.35 / - / 13.43
Final drive	:1	5.76

PERFORMANCE
Top speed: 181 km/h
Acceleration 0-100 km/h: 10.9 s
In-gear acceleration 80-120 km/h (IV/V/VI): 11.9 / 14.9 s

FUEL CONSUMPTION
Urban: 9.6 l/100 km
Extra-urban: 5.2 l/100 km
Combined: 6.8 l/100 km
CO_2 emissions: 164 g/km
Tank capacity: approx. 50 l

WEIGHT
Kerb weight EU: 1140 kg
Permissible GVW: 1495 kg
Payload capacity: 430 kg
Max. permissible axle load front/rear: 870/730 kg
Towing capacity (braked trailer) up to a gradient of 12%: 650 kg
Max. roof load: 75 kg

Length/width/height (mm): 3635 / 1688 / 1416
Wheelbase (mm): 2467

WHEELS
Tyre size front/rear: 175/65 R 15 84 T
Wheel size front/rear: 5.5 J x 15
Rim type: steel

ELECTRICS
Battery capacity/installation: 46 AH/front
Alternator capacity 110 A, 1540 W

MINI One D

ENGINE
Cylinders/arrangement/valves: 4/in-line/2
Displacement: 1364 cc
Stroke/bore: 81.5 / 73 mm
Rated output/rated engine speed: 65 kW / 88 hp / 3800 rpm.
Max. torque at engine speed: 190 Nm / 1800 - 3000 rpm.
Compression ratio/recommended fuel grade: 17.9 : 1/ Diesel

TRANSMISSION
Standard transmission ratios:

I/II	:1	12.57 / 6.99
III/IV	:1	4.51 / 3.55
V/VI/R	:1	3.05 / 2,41 / 11,47
Final drive	:1	–

PERFORMANCE
Top speed: 175 km/h
Acceleration 0-100km/h: 11.9 s
In-gear acceleration 80-120 km/h (IV/V/VI): 10.1 / 11.7 s

FUEL CONSUMPTION
Urban: 5.8 l/100 km
Extra-urban: 4.3 l/100 km
Combined: 4.8 l/100 km
CO_2 emissions: 129 g/km
Tank capacity: approx. 50 l

WEIGHT
Kerb weight EU: 1190 kg
Permissible GVW: 1545 kg
Payload capacity: 430 kg
Max. permissible axle load front/rear: 870/760 kg
Towing capacity (trailer with brakes) up to a gradient of 12%: 650 kg
Max. roof load: 75 kg

Length/width/height (mm): 3626 / 1688 / 1416
Wheelbase (mm): 2467

WHEELS
Tyre size front/rear:175/65 R 15 84 T
Wheel size front/rear: 5.5 J x 15
Rim type: steel

ELECTRICS
Battery capacity/installation: 70 AH/rear
Alternator capacity: 130 A, 1820 W

MINI Cooper

ENGINE
Cylinders/arrangement/valves: 4/in-line/4
Displacement: 1598 cc
Stroke/bore: 85.8 / 77 mm
Rated output/rated engine speed: 85 kW / 115 hp / 6000 rpm.
Max. torque at engine speed: 150 Nm / 4500 rpm.
Compression ratio/recommended fuel grade: 10.6 : 1/ 91-98 RON

TRANSMISSION
Standard transmission ratios:

I/II	:1	14.4 / 8.33
III/IV	:1	5.48 / 4.11
V/VI/R	:1	3.51 / - / 14.07
Final drive	:1	5.76

PERFORMANCE
Top speed: 200 km/h
Acceleration: 9.1 s
In-gear acceleration 80-120 km/h (IV/V/VI): 10.5 / 13.5 s

FUEL CONSUMPTION
Urban: 9.7 l/100 km
Extra-urban: 5.3 l/100 km
Combined: 6.9 l/100 km

CO₂ emissions: 166 g/km
Tank capacity: approx. 50 l

WEIGHT
Kerb weight EU: 1150 kg
Permissible GVW: 1505 kg
Payload capacity: 430 kg
Max. permissible axle load
front/rear: 870/730 kg
Towing capacity (trailer with brakes)
up to a gradient of 12%: 650 kg
Max. roof load: 75 kg

Length/width/height (mm):
3635 / 1688 / 1408
Wheelbase (mm): 2467

WHEELS
Tyre size front/rear: 175/65 R 15 84 H
Wheel size front/rear: 5.5 J x 15 LM
Rim type: alloy

ELECTRICS
Battery capacity/installation:
46 AH/front
Alternator capacity: 110 A, 1540 W

MINI Cooper S

ENGINE
Cylinders/arrangement/valves:
4/in-line/4
Displacement: 1598 cc
Stroke/bore: 85.8 / 77 mm
Rated output/rated engine speed:
125 kW / 170 hp / 6000 rpm.
Max. torque at engine speed:
220 Nm / 4000 rpm.
Compression ratio/recommended
fuel grade: 8.3 : 1 / 91-98 RON

TRANSMISSION
Standard transmission ratios:
I/II	:1	12.79 / 7.79
III/IV	:1	5.65 / 4.62
V/VI/R	:1	3.83 / 3.13 / 11.94
Final drive	:1	3.68

PERFORMANCE
Top speed: 222 km/h
Acceleration 0-100 km/h: 7.2 s
In-gear acceleration 80-120 km/h
(IV/V/VI): 6.1 / 7.7 /10.5 s

FUEL CONSUMPTION
Urban: 11.8 l/100 km
Extra-urban: 6.8 l/100 km
Combined: 8.6 l/100 km
CO₂ emissions: 207 g/km
Tank capacity: approx. 50 l

WEIGHT
Kerb weight EU: 1215 kg
Permissible GVW: 1570 kg
Payload capacity: 430 kg
Max. permissible axle load
front/rear: 890/760 kg
Towing capacity (trailer with brakes)

---

up to a gradient of 12%:
Max. roof load: 75 kg

Length/width/height (mm):
3655 / 1688 / 1416
Wheelbase (mm): 2467

WHEELS
Tyre size front/rear:
195/55 R 16 87 V RSC
Wheel size front/rear: 6.5 J x 16 LM
Rim type: alloy

ELECTRICS
Battery capacity/installation:
55 AH/front
Alternator capacity: 105 A, 1470 W

MINI One Cabrio / Convertible

ENGINE
Cylinders/arrangement/valves:
4/in-line/4
Displacement: 1598 cc
Stroke/bore: 85.8 / 77 mm
Rated output/rated engine speed:
66 kW / 90 hp / 5500 rpm.
Max. torque at engine speed:
140 Nm / 3000 rpm.
Compression ratio/recommended
fuel grade: 10.6 /: 1 91-98 RON

TRANSMISSION
Standard transmission ratios:
I/II	:1	13.76 / 7.95
III/IV	:1	5.23 / 3.92
V/VI/R	:1	3.35 / - / 13.43
Final drive	:1	-

PERFORMANCE
Top speed: 175 km/h
Acceleration 0-100 km/h: 11.8 s
In-gear acceleration 80-120 km/h
(IV/V/VI): 13.5 / 16.0 s

FUEL CONSUMPTION
Urban: 10.0 l/100 km
Extra-urban: 5.7 l/100 km
Combined: 7.2 l/100 km
CO₂ emissions: 173 g/km
Tank capacity: approx. 50 l

WEIGHT
Kerb weight EU: 1240 kg
Permissible GVW: 1565 kg
Payload capacity: 400 kg
Max. permissible axle load
front/rear: 870/770 kg
Towing capacity (trailer with brakes)
up to a gradient of 12%: 650 kg
Max. roof load: -

Length/width/height (mm):
3635 / 1688 / 1415
Wheelbase (mm): 2467

WHEELS
Tyre size front/rear: 175/65 R 15 84 T

Wheel size front/rear: 5.5 J x 15
Rim type: steel

ELECTRICS
Battery capacity/installation:
55 AH/front
Alternator capacity: 90 A, 1540 W

MINI Cooper Cabrio / Convertible

ENGINE
Cylinders/arrangement/valves:
4/in-line/4
Displacement: 1598 cc
Stroke/bore: 85.8 / 77 mm
Rated output/rated engine speed:
85 kW / 115 hp / 6000 rpm.
Max. torque at engine speed:
150 Nm / 4500 rpm.
Compression ratio/recommended
fuel grade: 10.6 : 1 / 91-98 RON

TRANSMISSION
Standard transmission ratios:
I/II	:1	14.4 / 8.33
III/IV	:1	5.48 / 4.11
V/VI/R	:1	3.51 / - / 14.07
Final drive	:1	5.76 ·

PERFORMANCE
Top speed: 193 km/h
Acceleration 0-100 km/h: 9.8 s
In-gear acceleration 80-120 km/h
(IV/V/VI): 11.6 / 14.4 s

FUEL CONSUMPTION
Urban: 10.1 l/100 km
Extra-urban: 5.7 l/100 km
Combined: 7.3 l/100 km
CO₂ emissions: 175 g/km
Tank capacity: approx. 50 l

WEIGHT
Kerb weight EU: 1250 kg
Permissible GVW: 1575 kg
Payload capacity: 400 kg
Max. permissible axle load
front/rear: 870/770 kg
Towing capacity (trailer with brakes)
up to a gradient of 12%: 650 kg
Max. roof load: -

WHEELS
Tyre size front/rear: 175/65 R15 84 H
Wheel size front/rear: 5.5 J x 15
Rim type: alloy

ELECTRICS
Battery capacity/installation:
55 AH/front
Alternator capacity: 110 A 1540 W

MINI Cooper S Cabrio / Convertible

ENGINE
Cylinders/arrangement/valves:
4/in-line/4

Displacement: 1598 cc
Stroke/bore: 85.8 / 77 mm
Rated output/rated engine speed:
125 kW / 170 hp / 6000 rpm.
Max. torque at engine speed:
220 Nm / 4000 rpm.
Compression ratio/recommended
fuel grade: 8.3 / 91-98 RON

TRANSMISSION
Standard transmission ratios:
I/II	:1	12.79 / 7.79
III/IV	:1	5.65 / 4.62
V/VI/R	:1	3.83 / 3.13 / 11.94

PERFORMANCE
Top speed: 215 km/h
Acceleration 0-100 km/h: 7.4 s
In-gear acceleration 80-120 km/h
(IV/V/VI): 6.6 / 8.4 / 11.0 s

FUEL CONSUMPTION
Urban: 11.8 l/100 km
Extra-urban: 7.1 l/100 km
Combined: 8.8 l/100 km
CO₂ emissions: 211 g/km
Tank capacity: approx. 50 l

WEIGHT
Kerb weight EU: 1315 kg
Permissible GVW: 1640 kg
Payload capacity: 400 kg
Max. permissible axle load
front/rear: 890/800 kg
Towing capacity (trailer with brakes)
up to a gradient of 12%: -
Max. roof load: -

Length/width/height (mm):
3635 / 1688 / 1408
Wheelbase (mm): 2467

WHEELS
Tyre size front/rear:
195/55 R 16 87 V RSC
Wheel size front/rear: 6.5 J x 16
Rim type: alloy

ELECTRICS
Battery capacity/installation:
55 AH/rear
Alternator capacity: 105 A 1470 W

Timeline.

MINI does not exist in splendid isolation – though some fans might believe otherwise. Every model is embedded in the context of its time and reflects its own particular epoch. In typically MINI tongue-in-cheek fashion, the following chronological survey gives a taste of what else was going on in the world during the various MINI eras: in politics, lifestyle, design, music, architecture and film.

1959

MINI

— In August the British Motor Corporation (BMC) unveils a small four-seater badged as the Austin Seven and Morris Mini-Minor: the "MINI Classic" is born.
— After being lent a MINI Classic by its designer Alec Issigonis, John Cooper waxes enthusiastic about the car's racing qualities.

World affairs

— Fidel Castro along with Che Guevara and others seize power in Cuba.
— The Chinese occupying forces crush an uprising in Tibet and the 14th Dalai Lama goes into exile.
—The world powers usher in a policy of détente.
— The first hovercraft crosses the English Channel.
— The Soviet space probe Lunik 1 flies to the moon.

Music
— "Living Doll" by Cliff Richard and The Drifters remains at number one in the charts for six weeks.

Architecture

—The spiral-shaped Guggenheim Museum in New York, designed by Frank Lloyd Wright, is completed.

Design
— The hula hoop craze sweeps the world.

Fashion
— Barbie, the mother of all fashion dolls, is born.

The rest
— The first photocopiers come onto the market.
— *Ben Hur* features the most gripping chariot race in cinematic history.

1960

MINI

— January: the Mini Van.
— September: the Mini Countryman and Mini Traveller (pictured).
— "Mini Royale": the Queen takes a MINI Classic on a test drive through Windsor Park.

World affairs
— Richard Nixon and John F. Kennedy take part in the first televised debate during a presidential campaign. Kennedy is elected.

Music
— Ornette Coleman releases his LP *Free Jazz*, introducing the musical style of the same name.

Architecture

— The city of Brasilia, designed by architect Oscar Ribeiro de Almeida Niemeyer, becomes the new capital of Brazil.

Arts
— So-called Happenings are staged – provocative theatrical events inviting the audience to take part.

Fashion
— The first Doc Martens shoe – the Air Wair – is produced in Wollaston, England.

The rest

— More than 100 million television sets are in use worldwide.
— The contraceptive pill is introduced in the USA.
— Launch of the soap opera *Coronation Street*, the longest-running soap on British television.

1961

MINI

— John Cooper and his association with MINI lead to a historic development: the first Mini Cooper appears on roads and race tracks.
— January: the Mini Pick-up is launched.

World affairs
— The Berlin Wall is built.
— Soviet cosmonaut Yuri Gagarin is the first man to travel in space.
— A planned US invasion of Cuba is thwarted in the Bay of Pigs.

Music
— The Rolling Stones, Beach Boys and Bob Dylan launch their musical careers.
— Smash hits: "The Lion Sleeps Tonight" (The Tokens), "Hello Mary Lou" (Ricky Nelson) and "Let's Twist Again" (Chubby Checker).

Design

— The typewriter enters the electronic age with the IBM Selectric golfball model.

Arts
— The London exhibition "Young Contemporaries" introduces the public to a new movement: Pop Art.
— Joseph Beuys, Nam June Paik and Yoko Ono are among the artists in the Fluxus Movement.

Fashion

— Yves Saint Laurent, who made his name with designs for Dior, leaves the fashion house and launches his first own collection a year later.

The rest
— Bordeaux has an outstanding wine harvest and a great vintage makes its way into the cellars.

1962

MINI

— While the MINI Classic gradually carves out its own identity, the Austin Seven is renamed the Austin Mini.

World affairs
— The Cuban crisis. For days the world teeters on the brink of nuclear war.
— North Sea flood disaster.
— Telstar, the first communications satellite, permits live broadcasts between the USA and Europe.
— First exchange of Russian and US spies on the Glienicke Bridge in Berlin.

Music
— Record company Decca turns down the Beatles, claiming guitar bands have gone out of fashion.

Architecture
— The TWA Terminal designed by Eero Saarinen opens at John F. Kennedy Airport in New York. It is seen as a symbol of flight.

Design
— Robin Day produces his stackable polypropylene chairs.

Arts

— Andy Warhol paints his "Campbell's Soup Cans".

Fashion

— The pillbox hat becomes the latest rage after Jackie Kennedy wears it to her husband's inauguration in 1961.

The rest
— Europe suffers one of the coldest winter in 200 years.
— Marilyn Monroe dies on August 5th in suspicious circumstances.

1963

MINI

— The MINI Classic overcomes its seemingly invincible rivals, the massive Ford Falcons, to win the Alpine Rally.
— Going topless: Crayford Engineering in Westerham, England builds the first ever Mini convertible.
— Launch of the Mini Cooper S.

World affairs
— US President John F. Kennedy visits Berlin and makes his "Ich bin ein Berliner" speech.
— On November 22nd John F. Kennedy is assassinated in Dallas.
— John Profumo's affair with call girl Christine Keeler leads to the resignation of Britain's Secretary of State for War.
— The Great Train Robbery: Royal Mail's Glasgow to London train is held up and £2.6 million are stolen.

Music
— The Beatles have their first number one hit with "Please Please Me".
— Bob Dylan's "Blowin' in the Wind" becomes a popular protest song.

Design
— Kodak makes photography easier: the Kodak Instamatic 100 is the first camera to use a film cartridge.

Arts
— Andy Warhol sets up his "Factory" in New York, where he and his friends turn out numerous artworks and films.

Fashion

— The Beatles promote the "mop top" haircut, Elizabeth Taylor the Cleopatra look.

The rest
— The cassette recorder comes onto the market.
— "Weight Watchers" is founded in the USA.
— A new island named Surtsey emerges out of the sea following a volcanic eruption off Iceland.

1964

MINI

— The MINI Classic undergoes a major modification with the introduction of hydrolastic suspension, developed by Alex Moulton (withdrawn again in 1971).
— Paddy Hopkirk wins the Rallye Monte Carlo in a MINI Classic.
— Ferrari drives MINI: Alec Issigonis gives one to his old friend Enzo as a present.
— The first off-road MINI: the Mini Moke.

World affairs
— Nelson Mandela is sentenced to life imprisonment along with seven of his supporters.
—US space probe Mariner 4 reaches Mars and sends pictures back to earth.

Music

— Beatlemania: the pop group occupy the first five slots of the American singles charts.
— John Lennon buys a MINI Classic even though he hasn't yet got his driving licence.
— The "British invasion" reaches America with the arrival of the Rolling Stones, the Kinks, the Birds, Cream, Donovan, Van Morrison, The Who and other British bands.

The rest

— *Goldfinger* is the most famous of all Bond films, taking US$2.9 million at the box office in the first two weeks and making it into the Guinness Book of Records.
— Kodak introduces the Super 8 film format.
— Shopping is now carried in plastic bags.
— Joseph Weizenbaum of MIT works on the ELIZA computer program that simulates a conversation with a psychotherapist.

1983

World affairs

— Hamburg magazine *Stern* publishes the "Hitler Diaries", which later prove to be forgeries.
— The first democratic elections are held in Argentina.
— The Nobel Peace Prize goes to Polish trade union leader Lech Walesa.

Music

— Michael Jackson's album *Thriller* heads the US charts for 37 weeks.
— The MIDI interface for electronic musical instruments is introduced.

Architecture

— Building work on Trump Tower in New York is completed.

Design

— Sign of the times: Swatch wristwatches by various designers become cult items.
— Richard Sapper designs a kettle for Alessi.

Fashion

— Power look: jackets come with shoulder pads to match those in TV soaps *Dallas* and *Dynasty*.

The rest

— London football club Tottenham Hotspur is the first sports club to become a limited company.
— For the first time, global consumption of plastic exceeds that of iron.

1984

MINI

— To mark the 25th anniversary, the Mini 25 special edition based on the Mini Mayfair is launched in a limited production run of 5,000.

World affairs

— The Summer Olympics in Los Angeles are commercially financed for the first time.
— Indira Ghandi is assassinated by members of her bodyguard.
— A cloud of poisonous gas escapes from a Union Carbide pesticide factory in Bhopal, India, killing thousands.

Music

— Prince sells 10 million copies of the soundtrack to the film *Purple Rain*.
— Material girl Madonna storms into the charts with her hit song "Like a Virgin".
— Michael Jackson's hair catches fire during shooting for a Pepsi ad.

Architecture

— The Deutsche Bank Tower in Frankfurt am Main is completed.
— Prince Charles describes the planned extension of the National Gallery in London as "a monstrous carbuncle on the face of a much-loved and elegant friend".

Design

— Launch of the Apple Macintosh. "Mouse" and "window" take on entirely new meanings.

Arts

— William Gibson publishes his cyberpunk novel *Neuromancer* in which the word cyberspace is first coined.
— Tate Britain awards its first Turner Prize.

Fashion

— Filofaxes for yuppies, roller skates for everyone else in a hurry.

The rest

— Unknown manuscripts by George Orwell are discovered in Reading, England.

1985

MINI

— The Mini Ritz launches a series of special models based on the Mini City E that take their names from upmarket areas of London.

World affairs

— 17-year-old Boris Becker of Germany wins the world's most prestigious tennis tournament in Wimbledon.
— Mikhail Gorbachev and Ronald Reagan agree to work together in the event of an invasion from outer space.

Music

— "Live Aid", the biggest pop concert in history, is held in London and Philadelphia.
— Stars of rock and pop sing "We Are The World".

Architecture

— After a construction period of seven years, the Tashkent Tower in Uzbekistan is completed.

Design

— Michael Graves designs a kettle for Alessi.
— The designer drug crack is sold in New York for the first time.

Arts

— British advertising tycoon Charles Saatchi opens his art collection to public view.

Fashion

— Domenico Dolce and Stefano Gabbana set up their own company.
— Goth is in: fingerless gloves are not just for down-and-outs, and men can now wear black eyeliner too.

The rest

— The new CD-Rom has a storage capacity of 600 megabytes.

1986

MINI

— The five-millionth MINI Classic rolls out of the factory, making the MINI Classic by far the best-selling British car.
— The Mini Chelsea and Mini Piccadilly special models are launched.

World affairs

— Gorbachev tries to arrest the decline of communism through glasnost ("openness") and perestroika ("restructuring").
— Chernobyl nuclear reactor disaster.
— The space shuttle Challenger explodes.
— Prince Andrew and Sarah Ferguson marry.
— President Marcos of the Philippines is overthrown in a bloodless coup and flees to Hawaii.

Music

— The Rock'n'Roll Hall of Fame is founded. The first to be inducted are Chuck Berry, Ray Charles, James Brown, Fats Domino, the Everly Brothers, Buddy Holly, Jerry Lee Lewis and Elvis.
— Frank Zappa appears in an episode of *Miami Vice*.

Architecture

— The Lipstick Building in New York is completed.

Design

— The yellow smiley makes a comeback.

Arts

— Opening of the Musée d'Orsay in Paris.

The rest

— Spread of the first computer virus ("Brain").
— Halley's Comet makes another appearance after 76 years.
— The Soviet Union launches its MIR space station.

1987

MINI

— Twiggy, the iconic model of the sixties, features in another MINI Classic commercial.
— MINI comes full circle with the Mini Park Lane: the last London special edition is launched.

World affairs

— Margaret Thatcher begins her third term as British Prime Minister.
— Black Monday: the Dow Jones suffers its most dramatic drop of all time, plunging by 22.6 percent.
— A treaty between the USA and the USSR to destroy their medium-range nuclear weapons marks the reversal of the arms race.

Music

— Peter Gabriel's *Sledgehammer* videoclip wins nine MTV Music Awards.
— House music enters the UK charts for the first time: Steve "Silk" Hurley with "Jack Your Body".
— "Pump up the volume" by M/A/R/R/S popularises sampling.

Architecture

— Biosphere 2 is set up near Tucson, Arizona: an enclosed ecosystem covered in glass.

Design

— First conference on artificial life in Los Alamos, New Mexico.

Arts

— John Adams' opera *Nixon in China* is premiered in Houston, Texas.

Fashion

— The Order of the Garter, founded in 1348, now admits women as well.

The rest

— The five-billionth. human is born.
— The number of computers on the internet exceeds 10,000.
— German pilot Matthias Rust lands a Cessna on Red Square in Moscow.

1988

MINI

— Farewell to the creator of the MINI Classic: Sir Alec Issigonis dies on October 2nd, 1988 aged 81.

World affairs

— Golden Slam: Steffi Graf wins all four Grand Slam tennis titles as well as Olympic gold.
— Benazir Bhutto becomes Prime Minister of Pakistan, the first female leader of a Muslim country.

Music

— Michael Jackson moves into his Neverland ranch in Santa Ynez, California.
— Rock star Alice Cooper runs for Governor of Arizona.
— The first year in which worldwide sales of CDs surpass those of vinyl records.

Architecture

— The 13-kilometre Great Seto Bridge linking the Japanese islands of Honshu and Shikoku is opened.
— At 53.9 kilometres, the Seikan Tunnel is the longest in the world. Running under the seabed for around 23 km, it links the Japanese islands of Hokkaido and Honshu.

Design

— Golden Wattle (Acacia pycnantha) is declared the national floral emblem of Australia.

Arts

— *Rain Man* starring Dustin Hoffman and Tom Cruise comes to the cinemas.

The rest

— Acid house raves take over the clubbing scene.
— The first internet worm creates havoc.

1977

MINI
— Market launch of the Mini Special. Manufactured in Belgium from 1977 to 1981, it was only available in Continental Europe. It had a 1,098 cc engine, special wheel rims and a roof in contrasting colour.

World affairs

— A power cut brings New York to a standstill. It leads to looting – and a minor baby boom nine months later.
— Jimmy Carter is elected US President.
— Camp David: Israel and Egypt sign a peace accord.
— The US Senate approves funds to produce the neutron bomb.
— The Nobel Peace Prize goes to the human rights organisation Amnesty International.

Music

— Elvis dies at Graceland.
— The film Saturday Night Fever triggers a wave of disco dancing.

Architecture

— The Centre Georges Pompidou opens in Paris.

Design
— Trimphone launches the first pushbutton telephone.

Arts

— George Lucas revolutionises screen animation with Star Wars.

Fashion
— Disco music conquers the catwalks.

1978

World affairs

— Karol Woytila of Poland becomes Pope John Paul II.
— It's a girl: the first test-tube baby is born in Britain.

Music
— Bands such as the Boomtown Rats and The Jam usher in the New Wave.
— Kraftwerk release their album Man-Machine.

Architecture

— The "Gehry House" is built in Santa Monica.

Design

— Record players feature tangential pick-up arms.

Fashion
— New Wave blends the aggressiveness of punk with the Teddy Boy style of the fifties.

— Others opt for Lycra tracksuits as worn in the film Superman.

Arts
— First broadcast of Douglas Adams' The Hitchhiker's Guide to the Galaxy on BBC radio.

The rest
— Reinhold Messner and Peter Habeler are the first to climb Mount Everest without oxygen.

1979

World affairs

— The Shiite leader Ayatollah Khomeini returns to Teheran. Shah Reza Pahlevi flees into exile.
— Margaret Thatcher becomes British Prime Minister.
— Soviet troops march into Afghanistan.
– Mother Teresa is awarded the Nobel Peace Prize.

Music
— The first hip-hop records are released: "Personality Jock" by the Fatback Band and "Rapper's Delight" by the Sugarhill Gang.
— Top albums of the year: Sex Pistols, The Great Rock'n'Roll Swindle; Dire Straits, Communiqué.

Architecture

— The Xanadu House in Kissimee, Florida is designed to showcase the use of computerisation and automation in the home.
— The Europa Tower in Frankfurt am Main is completed.

Design
— Sony markets the first Walkman.
— Black & Decker launches its most successful product, the handheld "Dustbuster" vacuum cleaner.

Fashion

— Aerobics takes off with accessories such as headbands, legwarmers and role models like Jane Fonda and Sydne Rome.

The rest
— The Compact Disc, or CD, is introduced.
— Japanese car production exceeds that of the US for the first time.

1980

MINI

— The range still features the MINI Classic models Mini 1000 HL, Mini 1000 HL Estate (until 1982), the Mini City and the Van and Pick-up variants (until 1983).
— Production levels drop dramatically.

World affairs
— Ronald Reagan wins the presidential election.
— Mikhail Gorbachev becomes a member of the Politburo.
— Lech Walesa and supporters set up the independent trade union Soldarnosc in Gdansk, Poland.
— Start of the first Gulf War between Iraq and Iran.

Music

— John Lennon is shot by a deranged fan in New York.
— Buddy Holly's spectacles are "rediscovered" in a police file.

Architecture

— The Hopewell Center is completed, becoming Hong Kong's tallest building.

Design

— Millions of people exercise their minds and wrists trying to solve Rubik's Cube.

The rest
— Gourmets enjoy the "nouvelle cuisine", popularised by French chef Paul Bocuse.

1981

MINI
— The eighties see a wide range of MINI Classic specials come onto the market.

World affairs

— Prince Charles marries kindergarten teacher Lady Diana Spencer.
— Pope John Paul II is injured in an assassination attempt.
— In Iran, 52 American hostages are released after 444 days of captivity.

Music

— Launch of MTV.
— Austrian singer Falco becomes the first white rapper with his hit "Der Kommissar".
— Reunited: Simon & Garfunkel give a concert in New York's Central Park.
— The first of 9,000 performances of the musical Cats is staged in London's West End.

Design

— In Milan, Ettore Sottsass presents the first "Memphis" furniture collection in playful postmodern style.
— Launch of the British fashion and lifestyle magazine The Face.
— Luigi Colani designs a streamlined Citroen 2CV.

Arts
— The exhibition "A New Spirit in Painting" at London's Royal Academy showcases works of Neo-Expressionism.

The rest
— IBM launches the Personal Computer (PC) onto the market.
— The space shuttle Columbia takes off on its first flight.
— Indiana Jones embarks on his career as an archaeology professor-cum-adventurer.

1982

MINI
— The last two standard versions of the MINI Classic hold the fort in the eighties: the Mini Mayfair as the new top-of-the-range model (launched 1982) and the Mini City or Mini City E (launched in 1980 as the entry-level models). Both provide the basis for various special models.

World affairs
— Peace movement: millions of demonstrators around the world take to the streets to call for nuclear disarmament.
— Argentina and Britain go to war over the Falkland Islands.

Music
— Prince releases his double album 1999.
— Madonna gets 5,000 US dollars for her debut single "Everybody".

Architecture

— Dedication ceremony in Washington for the Vietnam Veterans Memorial designed by Maya Ying Lin.

Design

— Ridley Scott's film Blade Runner paints a darkly fascinating scenario of the future.
— Philippe Starck designs the interior of President François Mitterrand's private apartments in the Elysée Palace, Paris.

Fashion

— Leggings threaten to upset the aesthetic sensibilities of the general public.

The rest
— Japan sees the launch of a filmless camera that stores images electronically.

1971

MINI
— With production figures of 318,475 units, 1971 sees the best sales results in the history of the MINI.
— Hydraulic suspension is phased out.
— The Mini Cooper S is discontinued.

World affairs

— The environmental protection organisation Greenpeace is set up in Vancouver.
— Ray Tomlinson of the Bolt, Beranek & Newman company invents e-mail and uses the @ symbol to divide up the e-mail address.

Music
— The "Concert for Bangladesh" is held in New York's Madison Square Garden.
— At discotheques, emcees and rappers team up with DJs to hype up the dancers.
— Premiere of the musical *Jesus Christ Superstar*.

Arts

— Stanley Kubrick's *A Clockwork Orange* (see photo) comes to cinemas.
— Joseph Beuys, who expanded the concept of art by introducing materials such as felt and grease, along with political aspects, creates a public stir.

Fashion
— Vivienne Westwood, together with her husband Malcolm McLaren and Patrick Casey, opens the boutique "Let it rock at Paradise Garage" in London's King's Road.
— Hippies treat their feet to Clarks suede ankle boots, clogs or Birkenstocks.

The rest
— The US semiconductor industry congregates in a small valley south of San Francisco which becomes known as Silicon Valley.
— ARPANET, forerunner of the internet, comprises 23 computers.
— The first sperm bank opens in New York.
— Britain goes decimal.

1972

MINI
— The three-millionth MINI Classic leaves the Longbridge plant.

World affairs

— US swimmer Mark Spitz wins seven gold medals at the Munich Olympics. The Israeli team falls victim to a terrorist attack.
— In its report "The Limits to Growth", the Club of Rome global think tank forecasts that many of the world's natural resources will soon run out.
— Ping-pong diplomacy: US President Nixon visits China.

Architecture

— The Transamerica Pyramid in San Francisco is completed.
— The run-down satellite town of Pruitt-Igoe in St Louis, Missouri is demolished. The video of the demolition is used in the 1983 film *Koyaanisqatsi*.

Design
— Executives favour spectacles by Rodenstock.

Fashion
— *Cosmopolitan* – the women's lifestyle, sex and fashion bible – arrives in Britain after its successful launch in the USA.

The rest

— Bernardo Bertolucci's *Last Tango in Paris*, starring Marlon Brando and Maria Schneider, shocks audiences with its explicit sex scenes.
— Noland Bushnell invents the first video game, called "Pong".
— A consortium of British, French, Spanish and German companies builds the European wide-bodied Airbus A 300.

1973

World affairs
— An oil embargo imposed by Arab states leads to the world's first oil crisis.
— Yom Kippur war.
— The military junta in Greece is overthrown.
— General Pinochet seizes power in Chile.

Music
— Kool DJ Herc is the first disc jockey to repeat only the percussion breaks of funk, soul and disco music, laying the foundations of hip-hop. Young boys perform breakdance at his block parties.

Architecture

— The Twin Towers of the World Trade Center in Manhattan are completed.

— Opening of the Sydney Opera House designed by Jørn Utzon.
— At 443 metres, the Sears Tower in Chicago is the world's tallest building.

Arts
— Erica Jong publishes her erotic novel *Fear of Flying*.

Fashion

— Mick Jagger is voted "Best Dressed Man of the Year".
— The Afro look and tattoos make their mark.

The rest
— Israeli psychic Uri Geller bends spoons on television.
— The first international ARPANET connections go into England and Norway.
— Frenchman Henri Rochetain spends 185 days on a 120-metre rope at a height of 25 metres.

1974

World affairs

— Yassir Arafat addresses the UN General Assembly.
— Two *Washington Post* reporters uncover the Watergate scandal. President Nixon resigns from office.
— Henry Kissinger embarks on his shuttle diplomacy.
— The Portuguese dictatorship is overthrown in the "Carnation Revolution".

Music

— German group Kraftwerk, the world's first electro-band, release their classic album *Autobahn*.
— Top albums of the year: Genesis, *The Lamb Lies Down on Broadway*.

Fashion
— Vivienne Westwood renames her London boutique "Sex".

The rest

— Comeback: Muhammad Ali defeats George Foreman, seven years his junior, in Kinshasa.

— Belgian cyclist Eddy Merckx wins the Tour de France and the Giro d'Italia for the fifth time.

1975

World affairs

— Helicopters evacuate the last South Vietnamese allies from the roof of the US Embassy.
— The Nobel Peace Prize goes to Andrei Sakharov.

Music
— Premiere performance of the musical *A Chorus Line*.
— Top albums of the year: Patti Smith, *Horses*; Supertramp, *Crisis? What Crisis?*; Joni Mitchell, *The Hissing of Summer Lawns*.
— Rock group Queen produce the first videoclip in music history for their single "Bohemian Rhapsody".

Architecture

— Completion of the "Frank House" (House VI) in Cornwall, Connecticut, designed by Peter Eisenman.

Arts

— Steven Spielberg's blockbuster *Jaws* sweeps the beaches clean.

Fashion
— The UN declares the "International Year of the Woman".

The rest
— Two schoolfriends, Paul Allen and Bill Gates, set up a computer company in Albuquerque, New Mexico.
— IBM launches the first laser printer, the 3800.
— The IBM punch card becomes a symbol of the computer age.

1976

MINI
— The Mini Limited Edition 1000 rolls off the assembly line, to be followed by numerous special editions that become firm fixtures of the product portfolio.

World affairs
— The Queen sends an e-mail from the USA to England.
— 1.5 million Chinese attend the funeral of Mao Zedong, founder of the People's Republic.
— End of the Chinese Cultural Revolution (1966-1976).

Music

— "Anarchy in the U.K.", the first single by the Sex Pistols, puts punk on the map.
— DJ Grand Wizard Theodore invents scratching.

Architecture
— Architectural critic Charles Jencks popularises the expression "postmodernism" to describe a mixture of architectural styles.
— The Royal National Theatre in London opens its doors.

Arts
— Robert Pirsig's book *Zen and the Art of Motorcycle Maintenance* is a blend of Western and Eastern philosophy.

Fashion

— Safety pins, studs and spikes reign: punk is all the rage.

The rest

— British Airways and Air France launch a regular service with the supersonic passenger aircraft Concorde.
— The US probe Viking I lands on Mars.
— Steve Jobs and Steve Wozniak set up the Apple company.

1989

MINI
— Rover celebrates the 30-year anniversary of the MINI Classic with the Mini Thirty based on the Mini Mayfair. It is produced in a limited edition of 3,000.

World affairs

— Fall of the Berlin Wall. Eastern Europe's Communist regimes collapse.
— George Bush is voted US President.
— The Chinese Army causes a bloodbath among peaceful demonstrators in Beijing's Tiananmen Square.

Music
— Birth of a new music style known as Tekkno, later spelt Techno.
— Madonna's *Like a Prayer* music video shows burning crosses, provoking a major controversy.

Architecture

— The architectural team of Coop Himmelb(l)au creates a spectacular office building in Vienna.

Design

— Philippe Starck designs an iconic lemon squeezer for Alessi.

Arts
— Iranian clerics call for the murder of writer Salman Rushdie (*The Satanic Verses*).

Design
— Michelle de Lucchi wins the "Compasso d'oro" design prize for his desk lamp "Tolomeo".

The rest
— Physicist Tim Berners-Lee invents the World Wide Web.

1990

MINI

— The Mini Cooper is resurrected under Rover management.
— The MINI Classic provides proof of its endurance qualities, winning the Pirelli Classic Marathon with Paddy Hopkirk at the wheel.

— A MINI Classic co-stars alongside Tom Selleck, Steve Guttenberg and Ted Danson in *Three Men and a Little Lady*.

World affairs
— Reunification of Germany; the Cold War is over.
— The Central Committee of the Communist Party of the Soviet Union relinquishes the party's monopoly of power.
— In Paris, NATO and the Warsaw Pact agree to end their antagonism.
— Saddam Hussein invades Kuwait.
— Nelson Mandela is released from prison.

Music
— Rob Pilatus of Milli Vanilli declares in *Time* magazine that he is "more talented than any Bob Dylan or Paul McCartney".
— The Fender Stratocaster that Jimi Hendrix played in Woodstock is auctioned for 295,000 US dollars.

Architecture

— Completion of the Bank of China Tower in Hong Kong, designed by I. M. Pei.

Fashion
— On her "Blonde Ambition" tour, Madonna wears a corset with a conical bra designed by Jean-Paul Gaultier.

The rest
— Microsoft Windows 3.0 is launched.

1991

MINI
— Spring is in air: the first MINI Classic with a catalytic converter is launched.
— German Rover dealer Lamm creates the first Mini convertible as a special model. Only 75 examples of the "Lamm Cabriolet" are built, but the idea lives on.

World affairs
— The USSR ceases to exist. Russia opens up politically and economically.
— Gulf War: US troops carry out their "Desert Storm" campaign.
— Boris Yeltsin becomes President of the Russian Federation.
— The World Wide Web goes online.

Music

— Nirvana release their album *Nevermind* with the hit single "Smells Like Teen Spirit".
— German DJs Sven Väth, Cosmic Baby, DJ Dag and others develop the new electronic music style Trance.

Architecture

— Canary Wharf Tower in London is Britain's tallest building.

Design
— Braun Oral-B, the world's most successful electric toothbrush, is introduced.

Fashion
— The rise of grunge fashion: a bit dismal, a bit punky, a bit expensive.

The rest
— "Ötzi", a 4,000-year-old male corpse, is discovered on the Italian Similaun glacier.
— American Phil Zimmermann publishes Pretty Good Privacy (PGP), the first encryption program available to the public.

1992

MINI
— After a production period of more than 30 years, the 998 cc version of the MINI Classic is phased out. From now on only the 1.3-litre model is available.

World affairs
— Yugoslavia disintegrates. Serbian troops begin their siege of Sarajevo.
— Riots break out following a video showing police in Los Angeles beating up the black motorist Rodney King.
— Serial murderer Jeffrey Dahmer is sentenced to 936 years in jail.

Music
— Snoop Doggy Dog launches his career.

Design

— Classic of ecodesign: Wilkhahn produce the "Picto" office chair, designed so that each individual part can be replaced.
— Former surfing pro David Carson takes over as art director of the magazine *Ray Gun* and revolutionises graphic design.

Arts
— Actress Marlene Dietrich dies in Paris.

Fashion

— Supermodel friends Linda Evangelista, Naomi Campbell and Christy Turlington – The Trinity – have a profound impact on fashion.
— David Bowie marries model Iman.
— Dreadlocks come into fashion among whites.

The rest
— The number of computers on the internet exceeds one million.
— Pope John Paul II revokes the Inquisition's charge of heresy against Galileo.
— Family scandals and a fire at Windsor Castle prompt the Queen to refer to her "annus horribilis".

1993

MINI
— Inspired by the success of the "Lamm Cabriolet", Rover launches its own convertible. Based on the Mini Cooper, it has luxury specifications and is the most expensive MINI Classic model to date.

World affairs
— Bill Clinton becomes US President.
— Writer Vaclav Havel is elected President of the Czech Republic.
— The WWW experiences a growth explosion of 341,634 percent.

Music
— Whitney Houston's "I Will Always Love You" sets up a new record by remaining at number one in the US singles charts for 14 weeks.
— Michael Jackson agrees to his first interview in 15 years – with Oprah Winfrey.
— The US Mail issues an Elvis postage stamp.

Architecture
— The Umeda Sky Building in Osaka, Japan is completed.

Design

— James Dyson introduces the bagless vacuum cleaner, the Dyson DC01.

Arts

— *Jurassic Park* marks a new dimension in computer animation.

Fashion
— The body piercing fetish enters the mainstream.
— Claudia Schiffer causes a scandal after modelling clothes by Karl Lagerfeld with embroidered Koranic verses.

The rest
— The White House has an internet address: www.white-house.gov
— A bomb explodes in the underground car park of the World Trade Center's north tower, killing six people.
— id Software launches the computer game "Doom".

1994

MINI

— 35 years after the "birth" of the first MINI Classic, Rover launches the Mini 35 special edition.
— 30 years after his unforgettable triumph, Paddy Hopkirk takes part in the Monte Carlo Rally again in a MINI Classic – once again as number 37.
— MINI joins BMW: on January 29th, 1994, BMW buys out the British company Rover.

World affairs
— Michael Schumacher wins his first Formula One world championship.
— The Tutsi in Rwanda are victims of a genocide.

Music
— Led among others by MINI Classic driver Noel Gallagher of Oasis, Britpop goes into top gear.
— Nirvana frontman Kurt Cobain commits suicide.

Architecture
— The Channel Tunnel links Britain and France.

Design

— Herman Miller introduces his "Aeron Chair" to the (new) market. In the late nineties, this ergonomic office chair becomes a symbol of the boom and bust of the dot-com industry.
— The Netscape web browser spreads like wildfire.

Arts
— Steven Spielberg's Holocaust film *Schindler's List* is awarded seven Oscars.

Fashion
— Tom Ford moves to Gucci in Milan as creative director and fashion takes on a new gloss.
— Welcome to Prozac, Wonder Bra and Kate Moss, the icon of heroin chic.

The rest
— The Kodak DC-40 is the first digital camera on the market.
— Formula One racing driver Ayrton Senna is killed in a crash.

1965

MINI

— Time to relax: the first MINI Classic with automatic transmission enters the marketplace.
— Timo Mäkinen wins the Monte Carlo Rally in a MINI Classic.
— Barely six years after its launch, Alec Issigonis drives the one-millionth MINI Classic off the assembly line.
— For the woman who has everything: Peter Sellers gives his wife Britt Ekland a MINI Classic for her birthday.

World affairs

— Cosmonaut Alexei Leonov is the first man to walk in space.
— Students in Washington demonstrate against the US bombardment of North Vietnam.
— Race riots break out in Los Angeles.

Music

— Trumpet player Louis Armstrong makes a guest appearance in East Berlin.
— The Beatles are the first band to be awarded an OBE.

Architecture

— Opening of the Mont Blanc Tunnel linking France and Italy and measuring almost 12 kilometres in length.

Fashion

— Mary Quant sells miniskirts and dresses in her Bazaar boutique in London and becomes a fashion icon herself. The style is quickly dubbed the Chelsea look.

The rest

— The programming language BASIC is created.
— Two computers are connected via a telephone line for the first time, in a move which will eventually lead to the internet.
— The first container ship is built in Britain.
— *Life* magazine in the US publishes the first photos of an embryo in the womb.

1966

MINI

— You win some, you lose some: a MINI Classic wins the Monte Carlo Rally – only to be disqualified for allegedly having headlamps that contravened the regulations.

World affairs

— In China the Great Proletarian Cultural Revolution gets underway.
— Indira Gandhi becomes Prime Minister of India.
— France withdraws from NATO.

Music

— So as not to be confused with Davy Jones of the Monkees, the young singer David Jones changes his name to David Bowie.
— John Lennon is quoted in a British newspaper as claiming the Beatles were "more popular than Jesus", leading to protests in the US.

Architecture

— Eero Saarinen's Gateway Arch in St Louis, Missouri is inaugurated – a vast concrete structure that soars into the sky.

Design

— Keyboards come into fashion for inputting data into computers.

Arts

— Michelangelo Antonioni's film *Blow Up* (which also features a MINI Classic) becomes a symbol of the swinging sixties.

Fashion

— Diana Rigg (Emma Peel) popularises go-go boots in the TV series *The Avengers*.

The rest

— The film version of *Doctor Zhivago* makes Omar Sharif an international star.

1967

MINI

— The Mk II series gives the MINI Classic a mild facelift.
— MINI triumphs for the third time in the Monte Carlo Rally, this time with "Flying Finn" Rauno Aaltonen at the wheel.
— Alec Issigonis is made a member of the Royal Society, Britain's most prestigious scientific institute.

World affairs

— Che Guevara is shot dead in the Bolivian jungle.
— The supertanker "Torrey Canyon" runs aground off the coast of Cornwall, causing the first major oil spill.

Music

— The Summer of Love takes off in the USA. You don't have to be in San Francisco to hear Scott McKenzie's call to wear flowers in your hair and come to the Monterey Pop Festival.

Design

— Danish designer Verner Panton's single-section plastic chair goes into production. The Panton era is born.
— US company Raytheon markets the first microwave for US$495. From now on your hamburger is ready in 35 seconds.

Fashion

— The film *Bonnie and Clyde* inspires a revival of 1930s fashion – poles apart from flower power.

The rest

— In Cape Town, surgeon Christiaan Barnard carries out the first heart transplant.
— The idea of the internet is hatched at a meeting at the University of Michigan.

1968

MINI

— The Mini Moke, among others, gets the chop as the model range is pared down.
— Production of the MINI Classic is transferred to Longbridge near Birmingham.

World affairs

— Soviet tanks roll into the Czech capital to put down the "Prague Spring".
— Martin Luther King is murdered in Memphis, Tennessee.

Music

— The musical *Hair* comes to Broadway.
— Cream give their farewell concert at the Royal Albert Hall.

Architecture

— London Bridge is sold and reassembled in Arizona.

Arts

— Stanley Kubrick's science fiction epic *2001: A Space Odyssey* captivates cinemagoers.
— Radical feminist Valerie Solanas attempts to shoot Andy Warhol. He is seriously injured.

Fashion

— Barbarella already launched space age fashion. Now it is joined by body art as anything superfluous, like clothing, is shed.

1969

MINI

— In addition to a visually updated version of the MINI Classic, the Clubman range is introduced. The MINI Classic becomes a modern small car for the seventies.
— In autumn, British Leyland begins marketing the MINI Classic, which BMC had previously sold under the Austin and Morris badges.
— The Mk II series and Cooper (except Mini Couper S) versions are phased out, as are the notchback saloons with the Riley and Wolseley badges.

World affairs

— Apollo 11: Neil Armstrong takes a small step for man and a giant leap for mankind on the moon.
— Richard Nixon becomes President of the USA. Millions protest against the war in Vietnam.

— 400,000 hippies converge on Woodstock in upstate New York for a three-day celebration of rock music, peace and love.

Design

— The Boeing 747 "Jumbo Jet" and Concorde take their maiden flights.

Arts

— Wind through the hair on Route 66: *Easy Rider* roars onto cinema screens.
— *Sesame Street* premieres on American television.

1970

MINI

— Better late than never: Eric Clapton returns the MINI Classic that George Harrison had lent him in 1967 after the filming of *Magical Mystery Tour*.

World affairs

— The image of German Chancellor Willy Brandt kneeling in front of the Warsaw Ghetto Memorial goes down in history.
— The Apollo 13 moon mission is abandoned after an explosion on board the spacecraft.
— American scientists create the first artificial gene.

Music

— The Beatles split up.

Architecture

— The "brutalist" style of architecture makes inroads with raw-concrete, bunker-like buildings relieved by design elements in bright colours.

Arts

— British duo Gilbert & George create performance art with public appeal out of conceptual art and Happenings.
— Alexander Solschenizyn is awarded the Nobel Prize in Literature.

Fashion

— Men's fashions get off the ground. The influence of Carnaby Street and role models such as Manchester United star George Best leads to men rejecting trousers with knife-sharp creases in favour of brightly coloured satin and silk.
— Hippies bring Afghan coats, Indian scarves, Peruvian ponchos and gypsy blouses into fashion.

1995

MINI

— Rover launches the Mini Balmoral, an exclusive special model.

World affairs

— Greenpeace activists occupy the Brent Spar oil platform in the North Sea.
— Serbian troops lay siege to the UN Safe Area of Srebrenica.
— Right-wing extremist Yigal Amir assassinates the Israeli Prime Minister Itzhak Rabin.
— O.J. Simpson is acquitted of murder.
— A bomb attack on the Murrah Federal Building in Oklahoma City kills 168 people.

Music

— Mötley Crüe drummer Tommy Lee marries *Baywatch* beauty Pamela Anderson.

Architecture

— Opening of the San Francisco Museum of Modern Art, designed by Mario Botta.

Arts

— Christo and Jeanne-Claude wrap up the Berlin Reichstag.

Fashion

— Slogan T-shirts and alcopops are all the rage.

The rest

— *Superman* actor Christopher Reeve is paralysed from the neck down following a riding accident.
— The Dow Jones closes above 4,000 for the first time.
— Online services such as CompuServe, America Online and Prodigy now also offer internet access.
— Paul Flaherty creates Altavista, the first internet search engine, for Digital Equipment.

1996

MINI

— *Classic & Sports Car* magazine votes the MINI Classic the "Number One Classic Car of All Time".
— The 1,275 cc engine becomes the standard unit of the MINI Classic, which now also features multi-point fuel injection.
— The Mini convertible is phased out. Total production amounted to 1,081 units.

World affairs

— Machine beats man for the first time: the computer Deep Blue defeats world chess champion Garry Kasparov.
— Charles and Diana, Prince and Princess of Wales, get a divorce.

Music

— The Spice Girls launch their debut single "Wannabe".
— Phil Collins leaves Genesis, Madonna is pregnant, M.C. Hammer is bankrupt.

Design

— Larry Page and Sergey Brin begin development of Google.
— Toby Gard develops the computer game "Tomb Raider" for Eidos Interactive, along with the first virtual-reality sex symbol – Lara Croft.

The rest

— Dolly the sheep is the first mammal to be cloned.
— Aged 35, just one year younger than the MINI Classic, Carl Lewis wins his fourth Olympic gold medal in the long jump – his ninth Olympic gold medal overall.
— Battle of the web browsers: Netscape and Microsoft fight for domination of the internet.

1997

MINI

— 30 years after the last MINI victory in the Monte Carlo Rally, the Mini ACV 30 concept lines up at the start.
— Rover unveils its concept for the new MINI at the Frankfurt Motor Show. The development project named R50 paves the way for the new MINI generation.

World affairs

— The leader of the Labour Party, Tony Blair, becomes British Prime Minister.
— Princess Diana is killed in a car crash in a Paris road tunnel.
— China's grand old man Deng Xiao Ping dies at 92.
— Great Britain hands Hong Kong back to China.

Music

— Paul McCartney is awarded a knighthood.
— Elton John sings "Candle in the Wind" at Princess Diana's funeral.

Architecture

— The Guggenheim Museum in Bilbao is opened.
— The Petronas Twin Towers in Kuala Lumpur are completed.

Arts

— The "Sensation" exhibition at the Royal Academy in London marks a breakthrough for "Young British Artists" like Damien Hirst.

Fashion

— The Tamagotchis are here.
— British fashion designer John Galliano – spot the trademark pirate bandana – becomes chief designer at Dior.
— Gianni Versace is shot outside his Miami mansion.

The rest

— Jorn Barger is the first to coin the term "weblog".
— The first Harry Potter novel is published.

1998

MINI

— The MINI Classic makes it into the Guinness Book of Records: with a total production run of 5.3 million, it is Britain's most popular car.
— Fashion designer Paul Smith creates his own Mini Limited Edition. It has special blue paintwork and is striking for its elegant simplicity.

World affairs

— The Clinton-Lewinsky affair affords new insights into what goes on behind the doors of power.

Music

— David Bowie falls for the charms of the MINI Classic – and buys one.
— George Michael is arrested for "engaging in a lewd act" in a public toilet in Beverly Hills.

Architecture

— Hong Kong's Chep Lap Kok Airport designed by Sir Norman Foster goes into operation.

Design

— The colourful iMac designed for Apple by Jonathan Ive embellishes desks around the planet.

Arts

— Raymond Benson publishes his Bond novel *The Facts of Death*.

Fashion

— Kate Winslet appears at the Oscar ceremony wearing the Titanic dress designed by Britain's Alexander McQueen.
— Fashion guru Yves Saint Laurent withdraws from the Pret-a-Porter business.

The rest

— The free operating system Linux aims to compete with Microsoft Windows.
— Sony introduces the first Memory Stick.

1999

MINI

— Four decades old and as young as ever: the MINI Classic celebrates its 40th anniversary in Silverstone. The Mini 40 special is launched to mark the occasion.

World affairs

— The euro is introduced as a cashless currency.
— NATO begins air raids on Yugoslavia.
— Two students at Columbine High School near Denver shoot 12 fellow students and a teacher.

Music

— Jesse Ventura, Governor of the US state of Minnesota and former bodyguard of the Stones, declares February 15th to be "Rolling Stones Day".
— The Napster music file-sharing program changes the music industry forever.

Architecture

— Inauguration of the Jewish Museum in Berlin, designed by Daniel Libeskind.
— The Burj al-Arab Hotel in Dubai welcomes its first guests.

Design

— Apple introduces its iBook to the market.
— Development of the punk website MySpace.com, which launches on the internet in 2003.

Arts

— The sci-fi film *Matrix* packs in the violence and the audiences.

Fashion

— Red Bull, text messaging and folding mini-scooters are all the rage.
— Prada buys the majority stakeholding in Jil Sander AG.

The rest

— Julia Roberts and Hugh Grant put Notting Hill on the world map in the film of the same name.

2000

MINI

— The last of the MINI Classics leave the factory: the Mini Classic Seven, Mini Classic Cooper and Mini Classic Cooper Sport. For the German market there is still the Mini Classic Knightsbridge, but on October 4th, 2000 the time has come to say goodbye. The last MINI Classic bearing the number 5,387,862 rolls off the assembly line in Longbridge.

World affairs

— At the height of the dot-com boom the Dow Jones closes at 11,792.98, before the bubble bursts along with hundreds of internet start-ups.
— Vladimir Putin becomes President of Russia.
— George W. Bush is confirmed as the new US President one month after the elections.
— A Concorde crashes after take-off in Paris.

Music

— The Backstreet Boys perform in five continents within 100 hours.
— Madonna marries film director Guy Ritchie at Skibo Castle in Scotland.

Architecture

— After the opening of the Millennium Dome in Greenwich on New Year's Eve, the "London Eye" Millennium Wheel and the Millennium pedestrian bridge across the Thames are inaugurated.

Arts

— The Tate Modern Art Gallery opens in London.

The rest

— The final Peanuts comic strip appears.
— America Online buys Time Warner for 162 billion US dollars in the biggest merger in business history.

2001

MINI

— On the road again at last: the new MINI has arrived. The MINI One and MINI Cooper are unveiled before a delighted public. The MINI Classic has become the MINI.

— The first issue of *MINIInternational* is published.

World affairs

— On September 11th, four passenger aircraft are hijacked in the USA and flown into the Twin Towers of the World Trade Center and the Pentagon. The fourth crashes into a field in Pennsylvania.
— Swissair goes bankrupt.
— US troops march into Afghanistan.
— Enron goes bankrupt in the biggest insolvency case in US history.

Design

— Apple brings the music industry into the 21st century with its iPod.

Arts

— The terrorist attacks in New York destroy artworks worth around 100 million US dollars, among them works by Roy Lichtenstein, Alexander Calder and Joan Miró.

The rest

— The human genome is decoded.
— The free encyclopaedia Wikipedia goes online.

2002

MINI

— And then there were three: a sportier and more dynamic MINI Cooper S is let loose on the streets.

— The friendly face of the law – the German police force use the MINI as a PR vehicle.

— The MINI Collection celebrates its premiere.
— MINI sponsors the International Isle of MTV Tour for the first time.

World affairs

— Hamid Karzai heads the caretaker government in Afghanistan.
— The euro is introduced as a common currency into 12 states of the European Union as well as Andorra, Monaco, Montenegro, San Marino and the Vatican.

Architecture

— London's sleek new City Hall is inaugurated.
— The Bibliotheca Alexandrina in Alexandria is opened to the public.

Arts

— A sculpture by Henri Matisse (Reclining Nude I-Dawn) belonging to Madeleine Haas Russell is sold for 9.2 million US dollars.

The rest

— Michael Bloomberg is elected Mayor of New York.

2003

MINI

— The MINI One D adds a diesel variant to the model range.

— Drivers go to the limit with MINI Driver Training.
— Damien Hirst installs a "Spot MINI" on the staircase leading to the Saatchi Gallery in London.

World affairs

— Space shuttle Columbia disintegrates on its landing approach.
— An international group of volunteers flies to Baghdad to act as human shields.

Music

— Beyoncé Knowles launches her solo career with *Dangerously in Love*.

Architecture

— Daniel Libeskind's plans for the new World Trade Center in New York win the design competition.

Fashion

— Creative director Tom Ford announces he is to leave the Gucci Group.

The rest

— Oolong, the rabbit who could balance objects on his head, dies.

2004

MINI

— The "Always Open" era begins with the MINI Cabrio / Convertible that drops its soft top for the world.

— The MINI XXL, a six-seater stretch version, is presented during the Olympic Games in Athens.

— It's off to the race track: the MINI CHALLENGE is held for the first time.
— MINI gets a facelift.

World affairs

— The EU expands to take on ten new member states.
— A terrorist attack in Madrid kills 191.
— A seaquake in the Indian Ocean triggers a tsunami in which more than 220,000 people die.

Design

— SpaceShipOne, the first privately built rocket, reaches an altitude of 100 kilometres.

Architecture

— Taipei 101 in the Taiwan capital is completed – at 508 metres and with 101 storeys, it is currently the world's tallest skyscraper.

Arts

— Christo and Jeanne-Claude install "The Gates" in Central Park, New York.

Fashion

— Karl Lagerfeld designs an affordable collection for Hennes & Mauritz (H&M).

2005

MINI

— The MINI Concept is unveiled at the Frankfurt Motor Show.

— Bisazza decks out the MINI with 37,000 mosaic stones.
— MINI United in Misano, Italy attracts 6,000 MINI fans and their cars.
— Launch of the MINI Characters Park Lane, Checkmate and Seven.

World affairs

— The Israeli Prime Minister and the Palestinian President meet for the first time in five years. A ceasefire is agreed.
— Pope John Paul II dies at the age of 84.

Architecture

— The refurbishment of Crown Hall at the Illinois Institute of Technology begins with the smashing of a glass wall – a privilege that went to the winning bidder at 2,500 US dollars.

Design

— The Red Crystal becomes the new symbol of the International Red Cross and the Red Crescent.
— The Allianz Arena in Munich, designed by architects Herzog&de Meuron, is completed.

The rest

— The Swiss fuel cell-powered "PAC-Car" covers more than 5,000 kilometres on hydrogen to the equivalent of one litre of fuel.

2006

MINI

— INCREDIBLY MINI. THE NEW MINI: the latest MINI is launched in the autumn. It is even more dynamic, powerful and muscly than before. A new generation of engines guarantees that pure go-kart feeling, while the interior has been completely redesigned.

— The 218 hp MINI Cooper S with John Cooper Works GP Kit marks the launch of the fastest MINI of all time.

World affairs

— Germany hosts the Football World Cup. After a penalty shootout, Italy beats France to win the championship.
— Violence escalates again in the Middle East.

Music

— The 250th birthday of Wolfgang Amadeus Mozart is celebrated around the world.
— The billionth song is downloaded from Apple's iTunes Music Store.
— MTV turns 25.

Architecture

— Work begins in Manhattan on the Freedom Tower that is to replace the World Trade Center.

Design

— The 100-dollar laptop by Nicholas Negroponte is honoured in the Industrial Design Excellence Awards.

Arts

— Entrepreneur and MoMA President Ronald Lauder buys Gustav Klimt's "Portrait of Adele Bloch-Bauer" for 135 million US dollars – the most expensive painting ever sold.

Index

Figures in italics refer to photos

A

Aaltonen, Rauno 75, 84, 158, 164
ABS see Anti-lock Braking System
ACV 30 see Anniversary Concept Vehicle
Adaptive Transmission Control (ATC) 171
Adicolor 11
Adidas 11
ADO15 165
Aibo 13
Airbag 105, 171, 175
Aisslinger, Werner 15
Algues 21
Alvis 76
Ambient lighting 170
Ambient lighting 171
Ambrose, Tony 86
Amstutz, Gerhard (gee ly) 32, 48
Anastacia 138
Annabelle 48
Anniversary Concept Vehicle (ACV 30) 167
Anti-lock Braking System (ABS) 155, 171, 175
Apple 16, 24
ASC+T see Automatic Stability Control + Traction
ATC see Adaptive Transmission Control
Atkinson, Rowan („Mr. Bean") 147
Automatic Stability Control + Traction (ASC+T) 171, 175
Automatic transmission 171

B

Baladi, Lara 30, 48
Baumgartner, Fritz 163
Beatles 57, 63, 129, 145, 165
Beck, Jeff 80
Bisazza 140, 157, 162, 168
BMC see British Motor Corporation 77, 86, 165
BMW Valvetronic 173
Body colours 115
Bon Jovi 50
Bonnet-Stripes 162, 165, 168
Bouroullec, Ronan & Erwan 21
Bowie, David 53, 145, 157
Brabham, Jack 80
Braga, Marco 162
Brakes 171
British Leyland 83, 165
British Motor Corporation (BMC) 77, 86, 165
Bubble Cars 165
Burgstaller, Alexander 152, 158
Burton, Richard 98

C

Caine, Michael 145, 147, 166
Caine, Natasha 145
Campbell, Naomi 138, 142
Cargo Box 129
Carl's Cars 48
Carnaby Street 58, 61
CBC see Cornering Brake Control
Centre Speedo, 110
Chanel 66, 68
Chequered flag design 162
China Stylus 47, 50
Chloe 68
Clapton, Eric 58, 65, 80
ClassiCon 21
Claudel, Camille 49
Coded fob 174
Coldplay 50
Colour Line 117
Conran 68
Conran, Sir Terence 53
Contrast Roof 171
Cooper, Charles 80
Cooper, John 75, 80, 164
Cooper, Michael („Mike") 80, 83, 157, 158
Cornering Brake Control (CBC) 172
Coulthard, David 163, 165
Crash element 175
Crash sensor 172
Crash test results 172
Crow, Sheryl 50

D

DAB 172
dal Bianco, Carlo 162
Danner, Christian 152
Das Magazin 48
Day-Lewis, Daniel 53
de Vesto, Tom 14
Deformation zone 175
DIA 21
Die Toten Hosen 50
Diesel 142
Digilux 2 16
Dior, Christian 66
Direct fuel injection 172
Dirisio, Luca 158
DJane Sonique 158
Drive shafts 173
Driver assistance 113
DSC see Dynamic Stability Control
Dynamic Stability Control (DSC) 172, 175
Dyson, James 76

E

Easy Load System 172
EBD see Electronic Brakeforce Distribution
Ecclestone, Bernie 80

Electric steering lock 175
Electronic Brakeforce Distribution (EBD) 173
Elle Deco 48
EMS rail-guided transportation system 99
Engine 173
Engine, mounted near the center of the car 80
Eriksen, Sune 34, 48
Ernestomeda 10
Euro NCAP 172

F

FAI see Fondation Arabe pour l'Image
Ferrari, Enzo 145, 165
Ferré, Gianfranco 142
Filofax 53, 65
Fondation Arabe pour l'Image (FAI) 48
Fondation Cartier 48
Football World Cup 2006, Germany 135
Ford, Henry 76, 92
Frog Line 14
front-to-back 76

G

Gaia & Gino 23
Galliano, John 12
García Márquez, Gabriel 49
Gates, Bill 76
Gazzè, Max 158
gee ly siehe Amstutz, Gerhard
Gibson, William 64
Glass sunroof 173
Glasshouse 106
Global Positioning System (GPS) 174
Glue Boy 98
Gokart-Feeling 105, 112
GPS see Global Positioning System
Grönemeyer, Herbert 50
Gucci 60
Guinness Book of Records 133
Gursky, Andreas 48

H

Häberli, Alfredo 76, 79
Hack-Mac 24
Hadid, Zaha 10
Halm, Steffi 158
HANS (Hand And Neck Support) 155
Hardy, Don Ed 12
Hawthorn, Mike 80
Heated front windscreen 173
Heine, Achim 16
Heine, Olaf 44, 50
Herbert, Johnny 152, 154
Hill Assist 172
Hill, Graham 163

Homma, Takashi 28, 48
Hopkirk, Paddy 83, 151
Hulger 18
Hunt, James 163

I

i-D 48
Immobiliser 173
International Talent Support (ITS) 167
iPod 10, 16, 111, 168
Isetta 165
ISOFIX 174
Issigonis, Sir Alec 71, 75, 80, 113, 164
Italian Job Tour 157
ITS see International Talent Support
Ive, Jonathan 16, 65

J

Jacobs, Marc 18
Jagger, Mick 76
Jay FC 47, 50

K

Keepall 45 18
Key Memory 174
Key Reader 174
Kidrobot 12
Kloss, Henry 14
Kureishi, Hanif 53

L

Laffite, Jacques 152
Lang, Helmut 12
Lauda, Niki 163
Leather upholstery 117
Led Zeppelin 64, 65
Leica 16
Lestrup, Fredrik 152, 158
Liddon, Henry 83, 151
Life Ball, Wien 138, 142, 157
Limited Slip Differential 174
Ljungfeldt, Bo 151
Loewy, Raymond 105
Loftcube 15
London Mardi Gras 135
López, Marcos 40, 49
Lord Snowdon 80
Lord, Sir Leonard 165
Louis Vuitton 18, 24

M

Madonna 145
Magnum 49
Mäkinen, Timo 86
Mandarina Duck 14
Map DVD 174
Martin, Maxime 152, 158
Massaud, Jean Marie 23
McPherson front axle 174
McQueen, Steve 80, 165
Meller Marcovicz, Gioia 21

Mind-3-Software 13
MINI 9X 165
MINI body colours 166
MINI CHALLENGE 151, 158
Mini Clubman 129, 164
MINI Colour & Trim 114
MINI Concept 128
MINI Design 103
MINI Driver Training 162
MINI equipment combinations 166
MINI Exterior 104
MINI fan hotel 135
MINI Interior 110
MINI Logo 133, 165
MINI LOUNGE 168
MINI Mania 156
MINI Mucchio 156
MINI special editions 162
MINI Takes the States 156
Mini Traveller 129, 164
MINI United 156
MINI XXL 135
MINIInternational Photo Award 166
Missoni 142
Moffit, Peggy *72*
Montoya, Juan Pablo 163
Morabito, Ito 24
Morphscape 23
Morris, William (Lord Nuffield) 165
Moss, Kate 145
Moss, Stirling 80
Multifunction steering wheel 174
Multilink rear axle 174
Murakami, Takashi 18
Museet for Fotokunst (Copenhagen) 48
Myers, Mike 147

N
Navigation system 111, 113

O
Overboost 174

P
PAL 14
Parallelogram cinematics 128
Park Distance Control (PDC) 175
Parkinson, Michael *70*
Parr, Martin 42, 49
Passport 48
PDC see Park Distance Control
Penelope*Phone 18
Pink Floyd 57, 65
Pischetsrieder, Bernd 167
Playhouse theatre, Oxford 98
Plunkett Greene, Alexander 69, 72
Pop, Iggy 50
Pori Art Museum 48
Porro 23
Porsche, Ferdinand Alexander 76

Portobello Market 64
Poschardt, Ulf 76, 79
Potente, Franka 50
Purple Fashion 48
Purple Prose 48

Q
Quant, Mary 66

R
Radiator grille 104, 130
Radio Boost CD 172
Radiohead 50
Rain sensor 175
Rallye Monte Carlo 83, 98, 130, 151, 164, 167
Rashid, Karim 23
Ravaglia, Roberto 158
Ravensburger Spieleland 162
Rawsthorn, Alice 76, 79
Ray Gun 48
Reed, Lou 50
Remote key 174
Retro rules 18
Rindlisbacher, Franz 32, 48
Rindt, Jochen 163
robot garden 93, 99
Rodin, Auguste 49
Rolling Stones *63*, 163
Roope, Nicolas 18
Rosberg, Keke 153
Rosso, Renzo 142
Runflat Indicator 175
Runflat System Component (RSC) 175
Tyres 175

S
Safety Bodyshell 175
Safety Steering Column 175
Saint Laurent, Yves 66
Sanchez Brothers 36, 49
Sassoon, Vidal 66
Sellers, Peter 80, 145
Shrimpton, Jean *64*
Side-to-side 76
Smith, Paul 53, 130, 157
Sony 13
Spencer Davis Group 163
Sport Button 175
ST/ART 50
Starr, Ringo *69*, 80
Start/Stop Button 175
Stephen, John *61*
Steptronic 175
Stewart, Jackie 83, 163
Strahlung pur 156
Stuck, Johannes 152, 158
Summer Olympics, Athens, 2004 135
Supercharger 176
Surer, Marc 152, 158
Surtees, John 163

Swarovski 142
Swift, Russ 154
swissair gazette 48
Switch 48

T
Taylor, Liz 98
Technical Data 177
The Italian Job (Film) 57, 137, 145, 147, 154, 166
The Who *59*, 163
Theron, Charlize 166
Tivoli Audio 14
Truckercaps 12
Truffle 23
Tuning 176
Turner, Stuart 86
Twiggy *71*, 80, 145, 165
Twin Scroll Turbocharger 176

U
U2 iPod 16
Ünal, Ümit 38, 49

V
Valentin, Karl 49
Valve management, fully variable 173
Versace, Donatella 142
Visionaire 12
Vitra Switzerland 21
Vogue 48, *71*

W
Wahlberg, Mark 147, 166
Wall, Jeff 48
Ward, Mark 145
Warhol, Andy 83
Watt, James 79
Window box 128, 130

Z
Z.Island 10
Zanardi, Alessandro *157*, 158

Photo credits

The New Millennium.
p. 10/11: Zaha Hadid for Ernestomeda, Adidas Deutschland
p. 12/13: Don Ed Hardy, Visionaire Issue 45: MORE TOYS Blue Set, Sony
p. 14/15: Henry Kloss and Tom de Vesto for Tivoli Audio, Frogline / Mandarina Duck, Werner Aisslinger, Loftcube / Steffen Jänicke
p. 16/17: Jonathan Ive for Apple, Achim Heine for Leica
p. 18/19: Laurant Bremaud / LB Production / Takashi Murakami for Louis Vuitton, Hulger
p. 20/21: Andreas Sütterlin / Paul Tahon and Ronan Bouroullec, Gioia Meller Marcovicz for Classicon Deutschland
p. 22/23: Jean Marie Massaud for Porro, Karim Rashid for Gaia & Gino
p. 24: Ito Morabito for Ora Ito

Around the World.
p. 28/29: Takashi Homma, Coordination: Roland Hagenberg
p. 30/31: Lara Baladi
p. 32/33: Gerhard Amstutz / Franz Rindlisbacher
p. 34/35: Sune Eriksen, Assistant: Bjorn Damhaug, Models: Cecilie Roer, Martin Staxrud
p. 36/37: Sanchez Brothers, Assistants: Elena Willis, Anny Piché, Magic Maker: Nick Vincent
p. 38/39: Umit Unal, Art Director: Asli Abbasoglu
p. 40/41: Marcos Lopez, Assistant: Pablo Saborido, Digital Retoucher: Luis Gaspardo, Production: Jessica Moziman, Styling: Lisandro Trevi, Models: Cesar Alamo (Captain), Federico Perez, J.C. Lopez, Damian Baudracco (Sailors), Alejandra Filomena (Lady)
p. 42/43: Martin Parr
p. 44/45: Olaf Heine, Assistants: Sacha Brown, John Maxwell, Production: Annabel Schofield, Assistant: Alicia Zumback, Styling: Luca Ognibene (Props), Lawryn Sample (Clothes), Hairstyling: Bertrand W, Makeup: Laura Mohnerg, Models: Alexis Broker, Peter Dykstra
p. 46/47: China Stylus

Paul Smith, Mary Quant, MINI and the Swinging Sixties.
p. 54/55: Daniel Stier, Paul Smith Ltd.
p. 56/57: Daniel Stier (1), Bettmann (1) / Hulton-Deutsch Collection (1) / CORBIS, BMIHT (1)
p. 58/59: Hulton-Deutsch Collection (1) / Bettmann (1) / CORBIS, BMIHT (1), Picture Press / Camera Press (1), Paul Smith Ltd. (1)
p. 60/61: Paul Smith Ltd. (3), Picture Press / Camera Press (1)
p. 62/63: Bettmann / CORBIS (1), getty images (1), BMIHT (2), K und K / Astrid Kirchherr (1), Picture Press / Camera Press (1)
p. 64/65: Hulton-Deutsch Collection (1) / Neal Preston (1) / CORBIS, Picture Press / Camera Press (1), Paul Smith Ltd. (1)

p. 67: Bettmann / CORBIS
p. 68/69: Picture Press / Camera Press (2), Bettmann / CORBIS (1), BMIHT (2)
p. 70/71: Picture Press / Camera Press (1), Hulton-Deutsch Collection (2) / Bettmann (1) / Condé Nast Archive (1) / CORBIS, Ullstein Bild (1)
p. 72: Mary Quant Ltd. (2), BMIHT (1)

The Legends.
p. 76/77: BMW AG Historisches Archiv, BMIHT
p. 78/79: BMW AG Historisches Archiv (3), BMIHT (1)
p. 80/81: BMIHT, BMW AG Historisches Archiv
p. 82/83: BMW AG Historisches Archiv
p. 84/85: BMIHT (1)
p. 86: BMIHT

The Oxbridge Race.
p. 89-97: Peter Guenzel, Assistant: Will Morgan

From the Original to the Original.
p. 118-127: Peter Hertel, Assistant: Matthias Schmiedel, Setdesign: www.heckhaus.de, Post Production: Foag

Inspired by MINI.
p. 141: Darren Alexander (1)
p. 143: Lifeball.org / Andrea Fabian (1)
p. 144: BMW AG Historisches Archiv (3), BMIHT (1)
p. 146/147: CINETEXT Bildarchiv (3)

MINI Community.
p. 152-155: Florian Jaenicke, Assistant: David Maupilé
p. 157: Christina Reiffert (1)

Facts & Figures.
p. 162/163: ATP (1), Hulton-Deutsch Collection / CORBIS (1)
p. 164/165: BMW AG Historisches Archiv (1), BMIHT (1)
p. 166/167: CINETEXT Bildarchiv (1), Remigiusz Pyrdol (1), BMW AG Historisches Archiv (1), BMIHT (2)
p. 168: Peter Hertel (1)

Timeline.
1959-1964: BMW AG Historisches Archiv (6), picture-alliance / dpa (4) / akg-images (1) / Paul Almasy (1), Bettmann (1) / Andy Warhol Foundation (1) / CORBIS, CINETEXT Bildarchiv (1)

1965-1970: BMW AG Historisches Archiv (5), Hulton-Deutsch Collection (1) / Mark E. Gibson (1) / CORBIS, Sunset Boulevard / CORBIS SYGMA (1), CINETEXT Bildarchiv (3), Büro Panton / Thomas Dix / Vitra Design Museum (1), picture-alliance / dpa (4) / akg-images / Paul Almasy (1),

1971-1976: picture-alliance / dpa (6) / akg-images / Brigitte Hellgoth (1) / Henning Bock (1) / KPA/HIP/Museum of London (1),

CINETEXT Bildarchiv (3), Bettmann (3) / Hulton-Deutsch Collection (1) / G. E. Kidder Smith (1) / CORBIS

1977-1982: picture-alliance / dpa (8) / akg-images / Keith Collie (1), CINETEXT Bildarchiv (3), Julie Mason / GreatBuildings.com (1), Roger Ressmeyer (1) / Bettmann (1) / Kevin Fleming (1) / Douglas Kirkland (1) / Derek M. Allan; Travel Ink. (1) / CORBIS (1) , BMIHT (1), Sottsass Associati / Vitra Design Museum (1)

1983-1988: picture-alliance / dpa (3) / KPA (1) / Hackenberg (1) / akg-images / Keith Collie (1) / Guenter Lachmuth (1), Swatch (1), CINETEXT Bildarchiv (2), Apple (1), CORBIS (1), Alessi (1), BMIHT (1)

1989-1994: picture-alliance / akg-images (1) / ZB (1), Gerald Zugmann / www.zugmann.com (1), Alessi (1), BMW AG Historisches Archiv (1), CINETEXT Bildarchiv (2), Travel Ink. (1) / Joe Giron (1) / Michel Arnaud (2) / CORBIS, Pierre Vauthey / CORBIS SYGMA (1), Wilkhahn (1), Dyson (1), BMIHT (1), Herman Miller (1)

1995-2000: BMIHT (3), Manfred Vollmer (1) / CORBIS, Cardinale Stephane (1) / LA Daily News (1) / CORBIS SYGMA, picture-alliance / dpa (5) / KPA (1) / Berliner Kurier (1) / ZB (1), Apple (1), CINETEXT Bildarchiv (1)

2001-2006: picture-alliance / dpa (3) / akg-images / Robert O'Dea (1), Apple (1), Robert McCullough/Dallas Morning News (1) / Louie Psihoyos (1) / CORBIS, ETH Zürich (1), Peter Hertel (1)